SCOOP

Praise for *Scoop*

"Jack Nelson was one of the journalists who were responsible for the collapse of de jure segregation. Southerners, born into a long-segregated society, ultimately recognized that system was indefensible and undesirable. Desegregation happened sooner because of the perceptive and persistent writings of first-class reporters like Jack Nelson."
—**Haley Barbour,** former governor of Mississippi

"This story is bold and brilliant—just as Jack Nelson was. We miss him and miss the open, honest journalism he practiced. Jack was one of that small band who told the country what the South was really like—at risk to his own life and limb."
—**Julian Bond,** Board Chairman Emeritus, NAACP

"It's impossible to write honestly about the civil rights movement without evoking Jack Nelson's sterling byline. In *Scoop*, you will learn about his friendship with presidents, his passion for civil rights, and how he always seemed one step ahead of the other great reporters of his day. This is a marvelous memoir full of wit, insight, and guts."
—**Douglas Brinkley,** professor of history at Rice University and author of *Cronkite*

"Hardscrabble southern by birth, hard-nosed investigator by nature, Jack Nelson was the best of the best—a reporter's reporter who gave ground to no one. *Scoop* reminds us of what journalism can be and what it always should be. Jack's enemies were legion; so were his sources, but the public interest he served outweighed them all."
—**Hodding Carter,** former publisher, *Delta Democrat Times* of Greenville, Mississippi

"Journalism is history. This book about the early life of Jack Nelson will give you new insights into reporting, the civil rights movement, government, and growing up in the South. Look at the chapter titles: The Meanest Town in the South, The Orangeburg Massacre, Ambush in Meridian, Sin in the Classic City, Harvard Man, and many others that will make you sit up in your chair. The wow factor is big."
—**Marlin Fitzwater,** press secretary to Presidents Ronald Reagan and George H. W. Bush

"As captured in his splendid memoir, Jack Nelson exemplified the very best in American journalism. There simply was no stronger, more tenacious investigative reporter in print or in television news. His reporting for the *Atlanta Constitution* and *Los Angeles Times* was world class. As Washington bureau chief, he led the *Times* to heights of excellence."
—**Tom Johnson,** former publisher, *Los Angeles Times*; and former chairman and chief executive, CNN

"Jack Nelson was a champion of 'openness' and held himself to the same standards he expected of government and politicians. It's not surprising, then, that he was the first journalist to allow C-SPAN cameras to capture an inside view of his Washington bureau. Jack was entirely comfortable letting the public see how the news sausage was made—a spirit captured once again in his revealing posthumous memoir, *Scoop*."
—**Brian P. Lamb,** C-SPAN founder and chairman

"Jack Nelson was an eyewitness to one of the most significant political and economic transformations of the twentieth century. He was also a daring reporter, unafraid to confront powerful political leaders who resisted that change with force. In writing this book, Jack shares a piece of southern, American, and journalism history that will inspire generations yet unborn."
—**Rep. John Lewis**

"Jack Nelson and my father had an interesting relationship that early on found them as spirited adversaries. I know that as time passed my father developed a deep respect and affection for Jack Nelson, and the correspondence my father had with Jack in his later years was very meaningful to him. *Scoop: The Evolution of a Southern Reporter* is riveting and will take the reader on a journey back in time as it chronicles social changes in our country and culture. Many of Jack Nelson's revelations in his writing, I believe, stirred the conscience of our nation."
—**George Wallace, Jr.,** author of *Governor George Wallace, The Man You Never Knew by the Man Who Knew Him Best*

"While he was given 'Scoop' as a nickname when a cub reporter, Jack Nelson grew to be a lion in journalistic circles by scoring one major scoop after another. He became one of the twentieth century's best—and most respected—reporters, and this posthumous memoir is testament to the moral force he brought to his profession."
—**Curtis Wilkie,** author of *The Fall of the House of Zeus*

SCOOP

Jack Nelson

The Evolution of a Southern Reporter

Edited by **Barbara Matusow**

Introduction by **Hank Klibanoff**

Epilogue by **Richard T. Cooper**

University Press of Mississippi / *Jackson*

www.upress.state.ms.us

The University Press of Mississippi is a member
of the Association of American University Presses.

Photographs are from the collection of
Barbara Matusow unless otherwise noted.

First printing 2013
∞
Library of Congress Cataloging-in-Publication Data

Nelson, Jack, 1929–2009.
  Scoop : the evolution of a southern reporter / Jack Nelson ;
edited by Barbara Matusow ; introduction by Hank Klibanoff ;
epilogue by Richard T. Cooper.
      p. cm.
  Includes bibliographical references and index.
   ISBN 978-1-61703-658-3 (cloth : alk. paper) — ISBN 978-1-61703-659-0
(ebook) 1. Nelson, Jack, 1929–2009. 2. Journalists—United States—
Biography. 3. Civil rights—Southern States—History—20th century.
4. Southern States—Race relations. I. Matusow, Barbara. II. Title.
  PN4874.N293A3 2013
  070.92—dc23
  [B]
                        2012020841

British Library Cataloging-in-Publication Data available

Contents

Introduction

—HANK KLIBANOFF

As a literary genre, the memoir has come under attack in the last couple of years, often justifiably. There are too many people with too few years, too few experiences, and too little to say taking too much of our time glorifying their fifteen minutes of fame—and every quarter-hour increment that came before and after.

But there are others whose memoirs capture the meaning and reveal the importance not merely of a life, but of a time. This is one of those memoirs, and it's one that is particularly valuable to have now.

Jack Nelson's story is, of course, about him, his life and his extraordinary newspaper career before he retired. His years as a gullible cub reporter at the *Daily Herald* in Biloxi–Gulfport, Mississippi, as a pugnacious Pulitzer Prize winner at the *Atlanta Constitution*, and as the archetype beat reporter for the *Los Angeles Times* in its Atlanta and Washington, D.C., bureaus put Nelson in the forefront of some of this nation's greatest domestic news stories since the Civil War.

But more than one man's journey, this is the revealing (and entertaining) chronicle of newspaper journalism in the fifty years before the business went into intensive care just as Jack was retiring.

This is not a sentimental scrapbook or a gauzy reminiscence about the days of gumshoes and glue pots. Jack has produced a rich memoir that is historically important in its portrayal of newspaper journalism in the evolving and emerging South of the twentieth century. That these stories were part of the life and journalistic development of someone who became as well known and respected as Jack makes this even more compelling.

Jack straddled momentous periods in southern and U.S. history, and his memories about the difficult circumstances, the contentious people, and the calamitous events that he encountered provide a fully grounded perspective on that history. Inside these pages, you see how Jack, from his earliest days, was shaped by the events and circumstances he faced at close range—war, unemployment, white supremacy, black rebellion, bullying, hypocrisy, unchecked power and demagoguery.

But that alone would not be a good reason to read this memoir; there are plenty of memoirs by people who grew up in times of war and violence, who had no plumbing or electricity, who had to confront drunk dads and comfort grieving mothers, who want to confess embarrassing moments.

What makes this even more valuable is who Jack was, and the role he played as an actor in that history. Jack, to good purpose, felt "reporter" was not a title but an entitlement to ask anyone in power or authority any question at any time; he felt similarly entitled to obtain just about any document he believed might provide answers that would bring knowledge and clarity to his readers.

In Jack's early years, when he was reeling off mind-boggling stories about corruption and abuse in Mississippi and Georgia, that hard-nosed, unapologetic sense of privilege, in the best sense of the word, distinguished him from many reporters and probably cost him some friends. But Jack had an old-school belief that a newspaper reporter who was content to just be on the front row of history, and who didn't get out of his seat and go behind the curtain in search of—well, who knows what one might find?—wasn't really doing his job.

So Jack was not a bit player in anything. He was, through his steely commitment to journalism, a creator of events, a generator of news, a history shaper. And he did it better than just about anybody. To see the way he cultivated sources—even the cop in the opening chapter who bullied Jack when he was fifteen turned out later to be a great source—is to see a master beat reporter at work. To see the way he parlayed a beating at the hands of a doctor into additional sources for his Pulitzer Prize–winning investigation into abuse, negligence, and corruption at the state hospital at Milledgeville, Georgia, is to see an indomitable spirit.

Wherever Jack landed, he found the corruption others missed, or, more likely, disregarded. He found it in anything-goes, lawless Biloxi; he found it in buttoned-down corporate Atlanta; he found it in the college town of Athens, Georgia. Jack turned his investigations of illegal gambling, liquor sales, prostitution, shakedowns, and corrupt cops into such a trademark that honest mayors and military base commanders who felt helpless to clean up their own houses called on Jack to expose the miscreants in their midst.

That same push for truth is evident in the way Jack tells the story of his relationship with Ralph McGill, the legendary editor of the *Atlanta Constitution*, a man he deeply admired. Hardly anyone ever tells a story that reflects badly on McGill, but Jack does. His account of McGill's pique at Jack's critical coverage of a friend of McGill's was a surprise to me and showed a side of McGill rarely seen.

Jack turns his critical eye on himself and looks back with great humor at his self-inflicted embarrassments. You will find Jack being duped, in print, by an impostor; you will see Jack helping police stop a man who was assaulting prostitutes by allowing himself to be dressed as a . . . well, read on. His story about serving on a coroner's jury and finding himself caught at the crossroads of right and wrong is a classic, cinematic account of a young reporter whose naivete drives his idealism but also makes him blind to how others might use him.

Jack sometimes looked back wistfully on what he believed was a shortcoming in his career—his late arrival to civil rights as a beat. My own feeling is that this was actually an asset. By the time Jack became a civil rights reporter, his investigative reporting skills were so well honed that he was able to bring investigative reporting to the civil rights beat in a way no one before him had. Even among the accomplished and courageous reporters attached to the civil rights story, Jack operated at a level well above his peers because of his investigative instincts.

The hallmark of Jack's reporting was his focus on the race-driven perversion of criminal justice in the South. His development of a white Georgia state official as a news source produced the records that provided irrefutable evidence of racism in the Georgia criminal justice system. (That Jack now reveals his identity is very interesting and may cause some discussions in the trade.)

The widespread nature of that perversion became even more evident with Jack's coverage of the Viola Liuzzo case (where an FBI informant turns out to have been involved) and, more dramatically, his breakthrough reporting on the Orangeburg massacre, where law officers participated in killing college students, then lied about it. Jack's stories, a book he coauthored, and now this memoir show how the lies echoed all the way up to the governor.

Jack routinely challenged the official line, and he did it armed with deeply reported facts. These were significant scoops that showed how white law enforcement, riddled with Klansmen and resistant to the FBI, operated against the best interests of the public it was there to protect, and how the FBI had difficulty controlling its own destiny in the South.

All of that was but a warm-up compared to Jack's phenomenal reporting on the collusion in 1969 between the FBI, Meridian police, and the Jewish community to lure two Klansmen into a plot to bomb a Jewish businessman's home, a plot that law enforcement hoped to intercept so it could arrest, or kill, the Klansmen. Even those deeply familiar with *Terror in the Night*, Jack's book on this bizarre and bloody episode, will find his behind-the-scenes account of his role illuminating and disturbing. And it is impossible to read it and not feel the excruciating pain Jack experiences from the ethical trap he lands in.

It is not insignificant that the tough reporting and tough questioning of the official line that was the signature of Jack Nelson's reporting became almost a contagion among reporters from Selma to Saigon and beyond. These reporters, with Jack in the forefront, had moved past the "on the one hand, on the other hand" type of reporting and found themselves informed enough to be able to report the truth even when it contradicted the official report. This was, in the nation's news history, a watershed time, and Jack was among its exemplars. Their influence derived from well-reported assessments they were professionally equipped to make, not from publication of their opinions.

Those assessments showed neither fear nor favor. Jack was not in anyone's back pocket. His reporting challenged George Wallace and his running mate, Curtis LeMay, just as it had challenged cops in Biloxi, doctors in Milledgeville, brothel owners in Athens, Georgia, the FBI in Selma, Martin Luther King Jr. as he pushed the Poor People's Campaign, and every occupant of the White House, including those who came raised on grits.

Jack, sadly, died before he could finish this work; he was about two chapters shy of finishing a first draft. But he had made a smart and propitious decision many years earlier that assured his memoir's survival: he married Barbara Matusow, herself an accomplished writer, who had heard all the stories, knew what he was writing and realized that the rest of the story lay in all the files and stacks of papers Jack left behind. She dug in, reclaimed the memoir, and finished it with perfect fidelity to Jack's voice, style, and story-telling skills.

One of my own life's most magical serendipities involved Jack: my first reporting job was at the *Daily Herald*, the afternoon newspaper in Biloxi–Gulfport, Mississippi. That is where Jack got his start.

When I arrived, folks were still talking about Jack. When I wrote stories about corruption in the longshoremen's union at the Gulfport docks, Jim Lund, an editor whose friendship with Jack went back to their high school days, lifted me from all earthly restraints with a passing remark that the stories reminded him of work Jack had done.

So when Jim came to me one day to say Jack Nelson was on the phone from Washington and needed me to do a favor for him, I was speechless. Then I took the call.

Jack was deep into the Watergate story, and the name of a Mississippian, Fred LaRue, had emerged in documents and interviews. LaRue was both a White House aide and an official on the Committee to Re-Elect the President. Jack needed a comment from LaRue about something, and needed me to find LaRue.

"You'll find him in Ocean Springs," Jack said. "He's got a place there. He'll be on his boat probably."

I found LaRue in Ocean Springs, at his place there, on his boat. I called out to him. "Who are you?" he responded, tersely.

"I'm nobody, but I'm here for Jack Nelson."

"I've got nothing to say."

"Jack wants me to ask you if—"

"I said I've got nothing to say."

Jack, I told myself, wouldn't walk away. I had to hold my ground and keep asking questions. "Yes, sir, but Jack thinks you might know something about—"

"Listen to me: I've got nothing to say. That's it."

This was not helping me help Jack. It wasn't even a good quote. I needed more. I couldn't tell Jack I got nothing.

"Yes, sir, I understand, but see, here's the thing, Jack's writing a story about you and wants to know—"

"I'm telling you, and I'm telling you for the last time," he said, his voice rising, "I've got nothing to say—and I've especially got nothing to say to Jack Nelson."

Perfect! The quote might not make the *Los Angeles Times*, I realized, but Jack will love the reference to him. When I called Jack, he just laughed. "Give me that again, Hank," he said, and I could tell he was smiling as he wrote it down. He was not as disappointed as I was. He was happy I had let LaRue know Jack was on his trail. Indeed, a review now of Jack's stories in the *L.A. Times* reveals to me that LaRue must have been moved to call Jack back that day because he was quoted in Jack's story in the next day's paper.

Over the years I got to know Jack much better. He was a dear friend and reporting buddy of Gene Roberts, my coauthor of *The Race Beat: The Press, the Civil Rights Struggle, and the Awakening of a Nation*. Jack was one of our readers of *The Race Beat* before the book came out.

In the days before Jack died in October 2009, we spoke and I reminded him of the LaRue assignment. He laughed, then added, "Yeah, my guess is that what LaRue really said was, 'I've especially got nothing to say to that goddamn Jack Nelson.'"

Thinking back, I'm sure that's exactly what he said. Jack got it right again.

SCOOP

Chapter 1

A TASTE OF INJUSTICE

MOTHER AND I WERE STANDING in the yard when a black sedan pulled up in front of our house, a run-down, two-story rental in Biloxi, Mississippi. We moved there from Alabama during World War II, when my father was assigned to nearby Keesler Field. Out of the car stepped a big, burly man dressed in a dark suit and gray hat. It was one of those murderously hot, humid days in Biloxi, and the detective was sweating profusely. He tipped his hat to my mother, showed a badge, and introduced himself as a city detective. Could he talk with me for a few minutes, he asked.

"Certainly, go right ahead," she said, so unconcerned she turned and walked back into the house. I wasn't concerned either. I was a fifteen-year-old high school sophomore, and while I had run into a couple of disciplinary problems in school, I had never been in serious trouble, certainly not with the police.

I was only about five feet, five inches tall and weighed about 115 pounds at the time, and I remember thinking the detective looked awfully big, which he was—a six-footer with a thick body and a neck that seemed as wide as his cheeks. But I wasn't scared, at least not at first.

As my mother closed the door behind her, the detective turned to me and said he just wanted to ask a few questions. "Come on and get in, we're gonna go for a ride," he said, opening the door for me on the passenger's side.

As we pulled away, he turned again and looked at me hard. He had a pinched expression, tight lips and narrowed eyes, and he kept using a dirty handkerchief to wipe away the sweat dripping down his cheeks. I thought he was creepy looking. As he drove down the beach toward downtown Biloxi, I desperately wished he would say something because I couldn't think of anything to say myself. Finally, about a mile from our house, he turned and looked at me again and said, "I guess you know what we got you for, don't you? You might as well tell me what you did with it."

Suddenly, I felt panicky. Maybe he wanted to ask me if I was involved in tying cans on the tails of some cats in the neighborhood. I hadn't done it and didn't like it when I'd seen some other kids doing it. Are you talking about those cats and the cans, I asked him.

"Don't hand me that shit," he shouted, glaring at me. "You know what I'm talking about, boy!"

When we reached the police station on the first floor of city hall he flung open the car door, grabbed me by the arm, and led me past the desk sergeant and into a small room with no windows. He ordered me to sit in a straight-back cane chair, then pulled another one over and sat directly in front of me, his face about a foot from mine. I was trembling all over. I had never seen anything more menacing.

"You know what we got you for," he said again. "You better tell me what you did with it."

I insisted I didn't know what he was talking about, and he clenched his fist and drew it back as if to punch me. I flinched and began to cry. He dropped his fist, but glowered at me. As scared as I was, I was mad, too. "If my daddy wasn't overseas he'd beat you up," I said defiantly. It was 1944 and my father was a corporal in the Eighth Army Air Corps based in England.

The detective laughed out loud. "If you know what's good for you, you'll tell me what you did with it. You know what I'm talking about, boy—the jewelry."

I swore I knew nothing about any jewelry and pleaded with him to let me go. But he just leaned closer to my face and glared some more. Finally, there was a knock at the door and a much smaller man, also dressed in a dark suit and wearing a hat, walked in. The big detective stood up and said, "He's all yours," then left, closing the door behind him.

The smaller detective smiled at me, patted me on the shoulder, and said the other man had meant no harm, that I shouldn't let it bother me, and that I should help them with a case they were trying to solve. He pulled up a chair and explained that a house not far from where I lived had been broken into and some jewelry had been stolen. Somebody had reported seeing me near the house.

Over and over he asked the same question: what did I know about the break-in and the jewelry? And over and over I insisted I knew nothing about it. Finally, the big detective came back. He led me down a darkened hallway and locked me in a large cell where half a dozen other prisoners who appeared to be drunk or hung over were sprawled on bunks. Now I was more infuriated than scared.

After a half hour, the menacing detective came back, opened the cell door, and said, without further explanation, "Come on, I'm taking you home. We know you didn't do it."

I felt relieved, but I was stunned and indignant that I could be treated that way when I had done nothing wrong. Neither the detective nor I said anything as he drove the three miles back to my house. He let me out and drove off without apologizing or even talking to my mother. I gave her a blow-by-blow description of what happened and insisted something should be done about the way I was treated. Usually, Mother was unflappable, but my account of the ordeal unnerved her.

With my father overseas, she hardly knew where to turn but finally went to Keesler Field and consulted a legal affairs officer. He told her she had grounds for filing a civil suit but suggested that with her husband overseas it probably would cause her more trouble than it was worth and advised her to let the matter drop. She did.

But for me it had been a searing ordeal—one that I would never forget. I told Mother that once I was big enough I would confront the detective and tell him off. It was the first of many examples of abuse of police power at the local, state, and national levels that I was to encounter as a reporter over the next half century, and it profoundly affected the way I would later react to such abuses and to instances of corrupt or abusive actions by government generally. Looking back, I guess you could say uncovering official malfeasance became the leitmotif of my entire career. It may sound grandiose, but from that moment on, I vowed that once I was a grown man I would not sit idly by and let a government official or someone with police powers subject me or anyone else to abuse without being called to account.

Respect for law and authority and for the policeman's role as a protector had been ingrained in me. But suddenly it became clear that in some cases a person might need to be protected from police, and that with all their power to do good or evil, law enforcement officers, of all people, needed to be held accountable under the law. So it was no accident that for most of my career, I chased stories that involved a miscarriage of justice in one form or another, whether it was exposing crooked sheriffs in Georgia, reporting on the struggle for civil rights across the South, or ferreting out wrongdoing by the Nixon administration during Watergate. The stories were very different, but they all came down to government officials abusing their power.

Ironically, I was to spend a great deal of my professional life not only exposing abuses of power, but working closely with police, the FBI, and other law enforcement officers—including the hulking Biloxi detective who frightened me as a fifteen-year-old. Like many another investigative reporter, I would frequently find it expedient to work both sides of the fence. I never did anything I considered unethical. But looking back, I realize there were occasions when I walked a pretty fine line.

Chapter 2

BIRTH OF A SALESMAN

HAD I NOT BECOME A REPORTER I might have been a hell of a salesman. When I was a kid, people used to call me a hustler—someone who gets the job done with dispatch. I bustled around with boundless energy as a teenage reporter for the *Daily Herald* (now the *Sun Herald*), but even before that, as a small boy, I scurried around selling newspapers and helping out at my father's fruit stand. There's no question in my mind that these experiences helped hone the skills I would later need as a reporter.

My career as a child salesman was a matter of necessity. I was born in Talladega, Alabama, on October 11, 1929—the month the stock market crashed. With money scarce, by age six I was going door-to-door peddling magazines—*Grit, Liberty, Collier's,* and the *Saturday Evening Post,* all long since defunct. At various times I also sold shoestrings, shoe polish, iodine, mercurochrome, and Band-Aids. What little money I made I turned over to my family, which many kids did during the depths of the Depression.

The funny part is I liked selling. Making a sale was as big a thrill for me as getting a scoop would be later on. Of course, I didn't realize at the time how much the two professions had in common. Both required working long, hard hours, getting out and meeting people, and establishing personal rapport. If it was a hard sell—whether it was convincing someone to buy a product or persuading them to provide information—you had to gain people's confidence, sometimes acting friendlier than you really felt.

I guess I was what you might call an operator—someone who resorted to the tricks of the journalistic trade. Out in the field, I played the Good Ole Boy, deepening my drawl and varying where I said I came from depending on circumstances. In Georgia, if I was in the backwoods talking to a sheriff, I never said I was from Atlanta—that was as bad as saying you were from the North. I would say I was from Decatur, which is a suburb of Atlanta. And the sheriff would say, "You all right, boy." If I was in Alabama, I'd say, "I'm from Talladega, sheriff. My grandfather raised eleven kids there." And the sheriff would say, "You okay, boy." In Mississippi, I was always from Biloxi, although I didn't mention not moving there until I was twelve. My Biloxi roots were particularly important in Mississippi, because so many people there were paranoid about outsiders at that time.

Being gregarious and enthusiastic helped too. That and an unshakeable belief in the rightness and importance of what I was doing. The latter, I believe, was the key to any success I achieved. If I had to push the envelope a bit to make the sale, say cozying up to a key source to get a document, I believed the end was important enough to justify the means. But pushing the envelope never involved breaking my word, burning a source, or stretching the facts. Tactics like that were definitely off-limits in my book, the same as they were and are for anyone who takes journalism seriously.

There were a lot of Nelsons in Talladega. My grandfather, John Alonzo Nelson, operated a small café next to the train station at one end of Courthouse Square. The father of eleven, he used to joke that when he figured out what was causing it, he stopped doing it. At the other end of the square, on Battle Street, my father, Howard Alonzo Nelson, ran a small fruit store for several years until he went out of business. I was named John Howard for both my father and grandfather but was always known as Jack. (Thank heaven I escaped Alonzo.)

My father was the one who showed me the ropes of selling. He would have me stand outside his fruit store when I was only seven or eight, sometimes late at night when Battle Street was nearly deserted, hollering the wares in rhyme:

> *The river's wide and you can't step it!*
> *You love our bananas and you can't he'p it!*

Or:

> *Pee-a-nuts. White in the middle, red on top!*
> *Makes yore lips go flippity flop!*

The guy in the next-door photo shop would stand in his doorway and call out silly ditties too:

Step up and have your picture took!
No matter who you are or what you are
We'll make you look like your favorite movie star!

That pretty much passed for entertainment in Talladega in those days. It was a small town with three cotton mills and not much else to distinguish it other than the Purefoy Hotel off Courthouse Square, where you could get a room and a meal during the Depression for $1.60. The Purefoy was noted for its food: Duncan Hines even listed it as one of the best eating places in the nation.

The town also had all-black Talladega College, established in the aftermath of the Civil War—what we southerners called the "War between the States." Otherwise it would never be known for much other than Bobby Jenkins, the "Talladega Thunderbolt," an All-American running back at Naval in the early 1940s, and later, the Talladega raceway—home of the famous Talladega 500.

My father, who left school after the tenth grade, was the gregarious type, popular around town and known for his ribald sense of humor. He would tell me the same raunchy jokes he regaled his buddies with before I was out of short pants. I loved tagging along with him. So did my brother, Kenny. People would see the three of us and say, "There goes Hiny, Little Hiny [me], and Tiny Hiny [Kenny]." For all his charm and ebullience, however, Daddy was not much of a success in business. After the fruit store closed he was unemployed during much of the Depression, and as MawMaw, my grandmother, used to say, he was "bad to drink." To get a bottle of liquor Daddy would traipse down to the local pawn shop with household items, going so far as to pawn Mother's iron and ironing board. With Prohibition still in force, he sometimes got in trouble with the law for drunkenness and brawling.

I still vividly recall crouching in a corner of our tiny living room, trembling with fright the day my father knocked down a detective named Shaddux who had come to our house to arrest him. Daddy was small but muscular, about five feet, seven inches and 135 pounds, and the detective was much larger. But Daddy pounded him to the floor and then sat on him. Other police finally arrived and subdued my father and carted him off to jail. My folks later told me my grandfather, who was well-liked and had connections, pulled some strings to get him out. The charges were eventually dropped.

My father was inclined to be pugnacious whether drunk or sober, and that wasn't the only time I saw him slug someone. Once, when I was in the second grade and we lived briefly in Birmingham where Daddy had landed a sales job, my brother, Kenny, who was only four at the time, was viciously attacked by a chow dog chained up in our backyard. We lived in an upstairs apartment of a duplex and the dog was owned by the man who lived downstairs. The dog surely would have killed Kenny had not a neighbor's maid driven him off with a broom.

As it was, Kenny was rushed to the hospital where they sewed up wounds on his face, ears, and throat with, as I recall, more than forty stitches, several just below his eyes. He returned from the hospital with his head swathed in bandages, only his eyes and nose uncovered. After Kenny came home I was standing in the hallway upstairs when the dog's owner walked up to the landing and told Daddy he had better not have any idea of putting the dog to death. Daddy was cold sober but so angry he knocked him down the stairs with one punch. Then he saw to it that the dog, after being observed to be sure it did not have rabies, was put to death.

Although not as rowdy as Daddy, I got in my share of fights. Two in particular taught me not to go around picking quarrels. The first occurred when I tried to hitch a ride by jumping on a horse-drawn wagon that passed by my grandparents' house. A boy about my size jumped on it ahead of me. He had a disfiguring knot on his head and I told him if he didn't get off so I could get on I'd put another knot on his head. He got off and gave me what we called a "good whoopin."

Another time I was sitting in the stands during an elementary school football game with my uncle, T. M., and a redheaded kid was sitting in front of me, partially blocking my view. I told him, "Hey, Red, move your head." He turned and glared and asked if I wanted to make something of it. He was a little bigger than I was, but no bigger than T. M., who was only a year older than I was, and I figured he would take up for me. So I accepted the dare and we went behind the stands. Red took the first swing and knocked me to the ground and jumped on me, while T. M. stood by and watched. "Boy, you started it and you got what you deserved," he later said. I went home with a bloody nose and hurt feelings but a lesson well learned. Although I got in a few more fights, I never again started one.

My father's drinking continued to be such a problem MawMaw once put cabbage juice in his liquor, hoping it would make him sick and give up drinking. He got sick all right, but he didn't let up on the booze. She later found a bottle of his liquor, and I remember watching her smash the bottle against the back steps while he sobbed, "Don't do it, Mama, don't do it."

For all Daddy's drinking and frequent bouts of unemployment, I looked up to him and don't recall ever feeling really deprived. Maybe it was because during the Depression most people we knew were in pretty much the same boat. We frequently ate at MawMaw and PawPaw's—nobody could match MawMaw's biscuits and gravy or her banana pudding. We also depended on government commodities, grateful for the flour, cornmeal, and dried peas and beans that the federal government provided to millions of poor people.

At the same time, I think Daddy's drinking made me responsible at an early age. I turned all my earnings over to my mother, knowing she needed the money to keep food on the table. With the first money I saved after going to work as a reporter, I bought her a little two-bedroom house—the first one she could ever call her own. Most of the time we had lived in small rented apartments. In one of them in November 1939, my sister, Barbara, was born. She was several weeks premature and so tiny—about two pounds with a head about the size of a softball—that word spread rapidly and people came from surrounding counties to see her for themselves. By then I was ten and my brother, Kenny, was six and we had to make repeated trips with our toy wagon to a lumberyard about a mile away to scavenge for scrap wood to use in a wood stove to keep her warm. It seemed like an especially cold winter, and I remember once pulling the wagon loaded with wood while Kenny stumbled along behind, crying and complaining he was cold. "Stop that blubbering, boy," I growled, trying not to show how miserable I was feeling myself.

I guess the nadir for the family came when I was in around the third grade and we lived in a log cabin without electricity or plumbing in a tiny rural area about six miles outside Talladega. This was about 1937, and we used candles and kerosene lamps for light and drew water from a well in the backyard. There wasn't even an outdoor privy. We peed in a deep gulley about two hundred feet behind the cabin and hung on the roots of a pine tree over the gulley when we had other business. For toilet tissue we used, among other things, pages from a Sears, Roebuck catalogue.

Daddy was selling insurance, or trying to, while we lived there, and once he was given a pig in lieu of payment, and the pig got loose. Mother used to love to tell how my father, who was in the midst of taking a bath, jumped out of the washtub covered in soap suds, and chased the pig up the hill in back of our house. The way she told it, Daddy came riding back down on the back of the pig, slipping and sliding all the way home.

Mother never thought that poverty and respectability were incompatible; she taught us good manners and the importance of putting your best foot forward. She always sent us to the local school in nearby Idalia in freshly laundered clothes, which she had scrubbed in the washtub, hung out to dry, and pressed with an iron heated on a stove that burned wood—gathered by us in the woods around our cabin. Lunch tended to be meager; she usually sent me off with two little sandwiches made with biscuits and fatback. One day I left my lunch bag—with grease from the fatback sandwiches showing through the bag—on a shelf in the cloak closet. At noon when we all started collecting our lunches off the shelf, I cringed when Billy Frieze, who lived on a relatively prosperous farm nearby, picked up my greasy bag with one hand, held it out in front of him, held his nose with the other hand, and said in a loud voice, "Oooh, whose is this?"

Billy Frieze always brought a big lunch bag containing several apples and bananas and a couple of sandwiches nicely wrapped in wax paper. And he clearly was disgusted by the sight of my greasy little lunch bag. I was so humiliated that I looked away and didn't claim the lunch as mine. But I soon grew hungry, and it made me furious with myself. I vowed then and there I would never again be so ashamed of being poor that I would go hungry.

For a while Daddy had a battered old Ford Model T, and he used it to travel around the Talladega area looking for sales work, occasionally finding temporary jobs. Once, when I was seven, he managed to scrounge up enough money to take the family in the Model T, which had no top, on a trip to Albuquerque, New Mexico. My mother wanted to go there since she had spent part of her childhood there. When it rained as we rode through the Rocky Mountains, we held up an old blanket over our heads to keep from getting wet. During the nights all four of us stayed in single one-room tourist cabins. And along the way to and from Albuquerque we would shop at grocery stores and then cook over open fires we built in woods and fields.

Once a fire Daddy built in a wooded area of New Mexico raged out of control and we quickly left as flames shot up large trees. We could see the smoke billowing for miles as we sped away as fast as the Model T would take us. An old photo I still have shows Kenny and me, dressed in our cowboy outfits, standing beside the Model T outside a New Mexico gas station with a sign saying, "Gas, 10 cents a gallon."

While it's true that Daddy had his faults, and plenty of them, he was so full of fun and had so many jokes up his sleeve that people who knew him found him irresistible. Certainly my mother did. She was not one to complain, nor was she the least bit materialistic, so the privations we suffered didn't appear—at least to me—to have much effect on her. She just had a naturally upbeat disposition.

My father and she were very affectionate with each other. I can recall numerous times being sent out for a loaf of bread and coming back to find the doors locked. I knew enough not to bother knocking. Much later, as an adult, when I read a little diary my father kept while he was overseas, I realize they had what I would call a real love affair. He wrote again and again about how much he missed her and how he longed to hold her in his arms. He even wore a little locket around his neck with her photo in it. He was clearly becoming more responsible around that time. While the younger men went out drinking at night, he wrote in his diary that he often stayed behind in the barracks by himself, doing other guys' washing for extra money to send home.

On the face of it, my mother and father did not seem that well matched. Though no intellectual, Mother had a keen intelligence, read a lot, and possessed a strict code of morality, including a reverence for the law. She taught us to keep our word, respect our elders, and treat anyone who came our way fairly and honestly. There was no "nigger talk" in our house, although I can't swear my father never told a racist joke. As for Mother, I don't remember her ever speaking negatively about what we then called colored people. But we lived in racist times and racist places and I suppose my family unthinkingly accepted segregation as the normal order of things.

The Ku Klux Klan was active in the Talladega area in those days, but I was completely ignorant about the Klan and its brutality against blacks and other minorities until years later. In fact I later learned that when the Klan was reactivated in the 1920s after a dormant period, William Joseph Simmons, a native of Talladega County, became the Klan's imperial wizard. Nor did I know anything about prejudice against Jews, another of the Klan's targets. There were few Jews and no synagogue in Talladega, although the leading business on the courthouse square was Goldberg and Lewis, the town's only department store.

Catholics were another Klan target, and Mother was a Catholic from Birmingham whose maiden name was O'Donnell. Catholics were scarce in Talladega, and the town had no Catholic church. My grandfather, the son of a Baptist minister, was also a Baptist and so was my father although he was not very religious. But when we attended church in Alabama, which wasn't all that frequently, we went to a Baptist church.

When we lived in the country I continued to sell whatever I could. I would pick wild blackberries and my father would drive me to Talladega where I went door-to-door selling buckets of berries. Finally, in late 1940, when I was eleven, Daddy was so frustrated by our hand-to-mouth existence in Talladega that we moved to Atlanta where he found work as a clerk in a drugstore. Right away I began hustling around downtown selling the *Atlanta Constitution*. After the December 7, 1941, attack by the Japanese, I ran up and down Peachtree Street yelling, "Read all about it, Pearl Harbor bombed. Two thousand Hah-whoy-an casualties." Mother liked to recall that I was in such a rush to get out and sell papers, I ran off without putting on a coat, even though it was close to freezing. As I said, I always did like to make a sale.

Chapter 3

BILOXI BOY

THE ATTACK ON PEARL HARBOR in December 1941 enraged my thirty-five-year-old father. Several months later, despite being the father of three minor children, he joined the U.S. Army Air Corps. He was assigned to Keesler Field, later named Keesler Air Force Base, for basic training in Biloxi, Mississippi. We moved with him and rented a small house in Biloxi in the old Seashore Methodist Campgrounds, about a block from the beach.

When we arrived, Biloxi had a population of about fifteen thousand, not including the thousands of soldiers at Keesler Field. It was postcard pretty—a sleepy, sun-drenched resort with a thriving seafood industry. The town was also an inviting target of hurricanes since it sits on a narrow six-mile-long peninsula, jutting eastward along the Gulf of Mexico. In those days, huge, ancient live oak trees draped with moss lined the principal highway—two-lane U.S. 90—as it skirted the waterfront.

There was very little sand beach when we arrived, just a few little patches in front of the Biloxi Lighthouse and several now-defunct hotels. The gulf was held back by a concrete sea wall. Then, during the 1950s, the federal government paid for enough sand to be pumped in to create a twenty-mile beach from Biloxi west to Pass Christian.

The lighthouse, built in 1848 of cast iron, remains a famous landmark that has survived every succeeding hurricane, including the disastrous 1969 Camille and the even more catastrophic Katrina in 2005. In 1865 it was the only public structure in the area to be draped in mourning after President Lincoln was assassinated. Normally white, it was painted black and remained that way for several years.

As that long-ago act of homage to Lincoln indicates, Biloxi did not fit the profile of most Mississippi towns. While racial segregation was strictly enforced, the town was in other ways a tolerant, easygoing place.

It was populated mainly by Slavs, Italians, and French Creoles who were drawn there by the fishing and shrimping industry. Most were Catholic, and they brought with them a more relaxed attitude towards drinking, sex, gambling, and other human frailties. Their surnames were definitely not those you'd find in the Delta—Galotte, Perez (prounced Pee-rez), Pitalo, Tibadeaux, Mladnich, Kovacavich, Baricev. We had a lot of Pisariches and Peresiches in town, and people used to say that when a branch of the Pisariches got money, they changed their name to Peresich.

People had colorful nicknames, like Meatball Randazzo and Noo Noo Cruthirds. As kids, we would stand around on the corner ribbing each other. I thought my friends were the funniest people on earth. Some of them actually might have been.

Biloxians touted their town as the "shrimp and oyster capital of the world." Huge oyster reefs and a large shrimp fleet provided a bountiful supply that was shipped all over the country. The town also attracted tourists during the summer months and hosted numerous conventions of out-of-town trade and professional groups year round.

It was an idyllic place to grow up. In the summers Kenny and I would get up before daybreak and go down to the old campgrounds pier near our house and paddle a skiff out about two hundred yards into the Mississippi Sound. We would anchor over an oyster bed in the shallow water and fish for several hours, returning with scores of white and speckled trout and, when we were lucky, flounder. Or we would take a couple of nets out on the pier, bait them with pieces of chicken or red meat, and catch a bushel basket of crabs by noon. You could cast into the shallow waters right off shore and in no time at all bring in a load of mullet—what we called Biloxi bacon.

While Daddy was undergoing basic training at Keesler, Kenny and I sold the New Orleans *States* and New Orleans *Times-Picayune* to soldiers at Keesler. We would search for stories that might lure them into buying the paper and then yell out a headline. I remember I once shouted, "Read all about it, soldiers' pay raise," but the soldier who bought the paper couldn't find anything about it. "Hey, kid," he yelled after me, "where's it say anything about a pay raise?" "Page 5," I replied. "State representative calls for soldiers' pay raise." "Little bastard," he shouted, as I hurried away, looking for the next sale. The way I saw it, I wasn't telling a lie. I was just pushing the envelope a wee bit.

Kids selling papers at Keesler frequently called soldiers from the North "damned Yankees," and they often referred to us as "little rebel bastards" sometimes joking, sometimes not. I didn't like it when they referred to the town as "the armpit of the world," either. Although it wasn't uncommon for soldiers to talk that way about towns near their military bases, Biloxi's humid mosquito-infested summers probably gave them a reason to dislike the place.

Soldiers from the South were always looking for ways to rib the Yankees. A southern soldier once gave me a quarter to yell, "Read all about it, nigger whorehouse burns down, five Yankees found dead." There were no blacks among the Keesler troops in those days, but my cry brought hoots of laughter from southern soldiers. "Damn little rebel bastard," the Yankees yelled at me. Although what I said clearly was racist, at the time it struck me that I had delivered a pretty hilarious line. I was so naïve and insensitive that it never occurred to me how offensive the remark was.

Racial inequality and segregation were so entrenched in southern life—accepted unquestionably by almost all whites and endured as impossible to change by nearly all blacks—that growing up in Biloxi I seldom heard the subject discussed as an issue. If the topic came up at all among polite people, it was usually referred to obliquely as "the situation." It wasn't until after the 1954 Supreme Court school desegregation decision that I began to hear a few references to what became known as "the nigger problem."

Blacks were less than 20 percent of Biloxi's population and they were concentrated in a small section of town near Back Bay. For the most part, they were employed as maids and laborers or held other minimum-paying service jobs of one kind or another. Social interaction between the races was minimal but generally nonconfrontational. (The apparent détente between the races would be shattered some years later, in 1960, when a group of blacks tried to integrate the rigidly segregated beach. They were set upon by a white mob swinging tire irons and clubs, and later that night, dozens of people, mostly blacks unconnected with the wade-in, were injured in drive-by shootings and beatings.)

In my day, of course, the schools—public and parochial—were strictly segregated, and the all-boys Notre Dame High School, which I attended upon reaching the ninth grade, was white, as were the Holy Cross brothers who taught us. Biloxi being heavily Catholic, my mother was finally able to attend a church of her own religion. She became a devout Catholic, attending Mass every Sunday and seeing to it that we kids did, too. I went to please her, but not much religion rubbed off on me.

Although we lacked money for tuition, my mother arranged for me to pay my way at Notre Dame by waxing the school's hardwood floors, shining the chandeliers, and washing the windows, which I did with my customary gusto. We lived about a mile away and I walked to and from school every day as I had to schools in Talladega and Atlanta.

Notre Dame opened in 1943, my freshman year, when I was fourteen. It occupied the old Dantzler Mansion, a stately white two-story structure on the beach across from the lighthouse. For the most part the Holy Cross brothers who taught us were no-nonsense teachers who put a high premium on hard work, discipline, and obeying the rules. If an infraction was serious enough, such as disrupting a class, punishment could range from a slap upside the head to detention hall to being ordered to clean up the school grounds. Today, teachers would risk criminal charges for doing what some of the rougher brothers did, but at Notre Dame, we students considered it routine, while parents generally supported a knock here or there as a way to keep their kids in line. If a kid got slapped at school and his parents learned about it he was likely to get slapped again when he got home.

Although some of the brothers could be overbearing, even the toughest students generally shrank from confronting them. But we groused behind the brothers' backs and devised nicknames for several of them. Brother Hyacinth, the square-jawed, tough-talking principal, was "the Jaw." Brother Eamon, a pugnacious little guy with a short temper who was given to smirking while slapping a student was known as "Eamon the Smiling Demon."

A new teacher, Brother Edgar, arrived at the school one day and we nicknamed him "Egad" and decided to test him. As he opened class several of us clicked our tongues on the roofs of our mouths to make a knock-knock sound. Brother Edgar looked around the room but couldn't spot the source of the noise. We did it again and he looked up and said firmly, "That'll be enough of that." We click-clicked with our tongues one more time and he brought both fists down on his desk with a thunderous sound that could be heard in other classrooms, glared up and down the five rows of students, and angrily shouted, "Okay, okay, the next guy who does it is gonna get it!"

My close friend Al Rushing leaned over and whispered to me, "You're chicken if you don't do it again." Taking the bait, I looked poker-faced straight ahead and click-clicked again. Brother Edgar bolted from his desk, red-faced and waving his arms, and shouted, "Who did it? Who did it?" The room was stone silent. Brother Edgar began walking down the first row questioning students one by one. "Garlotte, did you do it?" "No,

Brother." "Ladner, did you do it?" "No, Brother." "Seymour, did you do it?" "No, Brother." He went down the entire first row questioning every student and got the same "no, Brother" every time.

He started on the second row and suddenly asked, "Rushing, did you do it?" "No, Brother," my buddy said. My heart pounded as Brother Edgar stopped in front of me. But then he passed me by without a word and then went on to ask the same question of every other student on that row and every student on the final three rows—and he always got the answer, "No, Brother." Finally he started walking slowly back to his desk, then suddenly whirled around, pointed a finger at me, and demanded, "Nelson, did you do it?!"

My throat was dry, but I managed to blurt out, "Yeah, Brother, I did it." I cringed and other students looked on bug-eyed as Brother Edgar bounded over to my desk, grabbed me by the hair with one hand and pulled the other hand back as though to punch me. Finally, he turned my hair loose and said in a loud but even voice, "Guy, you sure are lucky I can hold my temper! See me after school." After school he lectured me about disrupting a classroom and told me I'd better not blow a second chance. I saw the wisdom of his lecture and thereafter got along fine with Brother Edgar.

My father returned to Biloxi at the end of World War II after serving almost two years in Europe and was honorably discharged as a corporal with a European African Middle East Theatre Ribbon and three overseas service bars. With other servicemen returning at the same time, jobs were scarce in Biloxi, and once again he found it difficult to find a job. He had been back only eight months and was still unemployed when the unimaginable happened. He was struck and killed by a car on a Sunday morning while walking across West Beach Drive near our house. He was only thirty-eight years old.

We had been so thrilled when he came back home from the war unscathed that it seemed doubly cruel to lose him so soon afterwards. It was particularly rough on my mother, who now found herself with three children between the ages of six and sixteen to support and no family in the area to lend moral or economic support. She took a job as book-keeper in a local insurance company which didn't pay very well, so she needed every extra cent Kenny and I could earn.

Oddly, I can't remember much about my own feelings when my father died, probably because I've always had a tendency to push unpleasant things to the back of my mind. At least that's what my wife, Barbara, tells me. In retrospect though, it's pretty clear I was deeply upset by Daddy's death. While I'd always been a cutup in class, my behavior became more troubling after he died—I began to behave insolently towards teachers and ignored homework assignments. The last straw, so far as the principal was concerned, came when I balked at a Latin assignment. I got thrown out of the classroom, then bolted from the detention room. Brother Hyacinth called me into his office and said, "Nelson, you've gotten to be a problem. We're going to suspend you for three days, and if you come back after that and apologize we'll let you back in. Otherwise, you're expelled."

After my confrontation with Brother Hyacinth, I left in a snit. I went home and told Mother I was quitting school and joining the merchant marines. She cried and begged me to go back to school and apologize. Apologizing never was one of my strong suits, but I did. So I was readmitted to Notre Dame and managed to stay out of any more serious trouble.

At the time, I never connected my discipline problems to my father's death. It wasn't until many years later, when I got my FBI file, that I began to understand what I must have been going through. After graduation, I had applied for a job with the bureau before deciding to stick with journalism, and my file contained a summary of an interview conducted by an agent with Brother Hyacinth. In his report, the agent quoted the principal as saying that "Nelson was at loose ends and in low spirits for a short period and did not act at all himself. But he quickly snapped out of this attitude and should be considered as one of the finest graduates from Notre Dame in recent years." Brother Hyacinth went even further, calling me "a truly outstanding boy, very ambitious, and possessing unusual promise . . . an unusually fine athlete and a very good student, highly regarded by the faculty at Notre Dame." It was high praise indeed for one who finished twenty-eighth in a class of thirty-two and got suspended and threatened with expulsion for misconduct.

At Notre Dame you might say I majored in sports while paying far too little attention to my studies. Although I was so skinny that other kids joked that if I turned sideways you couldn't see me, I was obsessed with sports and played on the school's football, basketball, track, and boxing teams, and one year I served as sports editor of the *Lighthouse*, the school newspaper. The size of the student body—only about 120 students—undoubtedly had a lot to do with why I was able to make the football and basketball teams.

As a five foot, nine inch 122-pound first-string quarterback in my senior year, I spent a lot of time under piles of much larger opposing players. As I limped off the field after a much bigger Gulf Coast Military Academy team crushed us 76 to 0, Brother Nivard, our athletic director, looked at me sympathetically, shook his head and said, "Nelson, you sure must have strong bones." I was resilient, though, and never got seriously hurt, and I had a burning desire to keep playing regardless of the odds against me or my team.

When the coach told me he didn't know what he would do for a quarterback the year following my graduation, I seriously considered failing in hopes of returning to play another year. I had done so poorly in school that failing wouldn't have been difficult. But word that I might fail on purpose in order to play another year of football quickly spread around school. Brother Hyacinth, "the Jaw," met me one morning as I walked down the hallway, and said, "Nelson, I understand you plan to fail and come back to play football. Nelson, if you don't graduate and you come back to Notre Dame, I promise you won't be playing any football."

I passed, barely, and my football days were over. But I continued to box for a while. In those days high school boxing was popular in Mississippi and Louisiana and I was a Golden Gloves champion, making it through three years of school boxing without losing a bout. That was partly because I was taller than most of my opponents at the weight we boxed and could keep them at bay with a jab. I also trained hard for matches and had good coaches. But my post–high school boxing career was less illustrious. I joined an amateur Biloxi team and we traveled to New Orleans to fight a team there. The New Orleans *Times-Picayune* headlined a story in its sports section: "Willing Jackie Nelson Meets Jolting Jock Ventrilla."

I had put on a few extra pounds and in order to lose enough weight to make the featherweight limit I spit out the window of our bus all the way to New Orleans. After weighing in and making the weight limit, I drank plenty of water, so I don't think the spitting left me too dehydrated or hurt my performance. But Ventrilla was undefeated and billed as the National Amateur Athletic Union bantamweight champion. And he fought like it. For almost two rounds he battered me around as if I were a rag doll. Although I never went down, I was slumped against the ropes in a corner, unconscious, when the referee stopped the fight.

The next thing I remembered after being pounded into that corner was raising my head from a table in a French Quarter restaurant and looking around and seeing my teammates. They told me about the referee stopping the fight. I obviously had suffered a concussion and had been unconscious for several hours. But I never saw a doctor, which would have been unusual in those days. My boxing days were over. I was eighteen years old and I had to get on with finding a job.

Chapter 4

"SCOOP"

WORKING AS A PAINTER'S HELPER at Keesler Field, going ahead of the painter with a handkerchief wrapped around my face, brushing away dirt and cobwebs from under the eaves of barracks wasn't exactly the job I was hoping to get after graduating from high school. But it paid thirty dollars a week and jobs were scarce in 1947. I grabbed it and held on to it for several months. Then, one day while thumbing through the *Daily Herald* want ads, I spotted one that read: "General assignment reporter wanted, knowledge of sports desired." The mention of sports caught my eye and I immediately telephoned the *Herald*'s Biloxi office.

Except for having been sports editor of Notre Dame's school paper, the *Lighthouse*, I had no journalism experience. But I had played just about every sport at school and pitched fast softball on an amateur team. My lack of journalism experience didn't seem to faze Cosman Eisendrath, the Biloxi city editor, who interviewed me. After all, Mr. Eisendrath, as I always called him, had started as a bill collector for the *Herald* at the age of nineteen after graduating from Biloxi High School, and he'd become a reporter shortly thereafter. He liked my enthusiasm and my assurances I could do the job—lack of self-confidence was not one of my weaknesses. He hired me on a three-month probationary period with the understanding if I did okay during that time I could stay. Otherwise I would leave with no hard feelings on either side.

Under his guidance I learned the rudiments of the trade, writing routine stories about accidents, civic club meetings, obituaries, and high school football games. My biggest thrill was covering sporting events, even if I mangled a metaphor here or there. I still remember my lead about a star runner on the Biloxi High football team who later played for Mississippi State. "Shouldering the burden of an injured ankle, Norman

Duplain ran for three touchdowns . . ." I wrote, thinking it was a pretty sparkling bit of prose.

At the time, Mr. Eisendrath needed me because he was the only other editorial employee in Biloxi—there was another city editor eleven miles up the coast in Gulfport—and he did all of the local reporting until I came along. As the weeks passed, he gave me more and more responsibilities until by the end of my probationary period I was covering city hall, the police department, and the federal court.

I had another great mentor in those days—Wilson F. (Bill) Minor, the New Orleans *Times-Picayune*'s Jackson correspondent, a handsome World War II navy veteran. We often found ourselves covering the same events, frequently conventions hosted by Biloxi hotels where speakers included U.S. senators and cabinet officers. Since I had so little knowledge of national issues, I would often turn to Bill and ask, "What's the lead, Bill?" And he would point out several paragraphs he thought should be at the top of the story.

For years, operating out of his office in Jackson, Mississippi, Bill has fearlessly exposed crooks, Klansmen, and race-baiting politicians. He has also been the go-to guy for just about every out-of-state reporter who has come through Mississippi to cover civil rights, generously giving all comers background briefings, names and telephone numbers of contacts, and, crucially, advice on how to stay out of danger.

Bill has remained in Jackson for more than sixty years, covering politics and civil rights, seemingly impervious to death threats and social ostracism. He finally got a measure of the national recognition he deserved in 1997 when he became the first recipient of the prestigious John Chancellor Award, started by businessman Ira A. Lipman in honor of his friendship with the late John Chancellor. But Bill was already a hero to scores of reporters. (I once had an argument with longtime *Boston Globe* correspondent Curtis Wilkie, who mentioned that Bill Minor was his hero. "No," I argued. "He can't be your hero. He's *my* hero.") Through the years, he not only helped me on many a story, but he became a close, lifelong friend.

Bill, like Mr. Eisendrath, was always properly dressed and mannerly, but in other ways the two could not have been more different. Bill was a boat rocker. Mr. Eisendrath was a civic booster and soft-spoken gentleman of the old school who preferred to avoid controversy. He spent most of his working hours in the office, usually with the phone cradled on his shoulder while typing notes rapidly with two fingers—he had a great network of contacts who kept him abreast of everything that was going on in town. In the evenings, he often made calls from his house, and he would come to work the next day with notes written on cardboard from laundered shirts, the backs of envelopes, and other scraps of paper.

He was short and stocky with graying black hair combed straight back, and there was a certain formality about him. He was never "Cosmon" to me—I always called him Mr. Eisendrath. He always wore a coat, a white shirt, and tie, even on the hottest summer days when temperatures soared above a hundred. Although he never explicitly told me how to dress, I admired him so much I wanted to please him, which meant I too always walked around Biloxi in suits soaking with sweat all summer. He acknowledged that it wasn't the most comfortable outfit in hot weather, but in his view, that was the way to dress when meeting the public.

About two weeks after he hired me, I was checking some traffic accident reports at the police station when a big burly man wearing a suit and hat walked in. I instantly recognized him but didn't know his name. Another officer I knew introduced him to me as Detective Henry Cook. I had never forgotten nor forgiven the detective who had bullied and threatened me, and now I remembered my vow that if I ever met him after growing up I would tell him off. But I thought the time was not right for a confrontation, and as we shook hands I said only, "Glad to meet you."

A couple of days later, I was asking him some questions about a murder case and he gave me a comment I used in a story in that afternoon's paper. He obviously liked seeing his name in the paper and took a liking to me and began calling me "Scoop," a nickname that stuck, at least in Biloxi.

At the police station about a week later, Cook looked at me with a puzzled expression and asked, "Scoop, don't I know you from somewhere else?"

The right moment had arrived. Looking him straight in the eye, I pointed my finger at him and said, "Yeah, you do. Three years ago when I was fifteen you bullied me and threatened me and accused me of something I didn't do. You said I stole some jewelry and when you found out I hadn't done it you let me go, but you didn't even apologize."

"Shit, Scoop," he said, "I didn't mean to do you no harm, I was just doin' my job. No hard feelings, I hope."

There may not have been any hard feelings on his part, but there sure were on mine. I pointed my finger at him and told him that if I ever saw or heard of him treating anyone else like that I'd put his name in the paper—on page one if possible. He said okay and we both let it drop. I never saw or heard of him mistreating anyone, and he became one of my most valuable sources. He continued to be known as an aggressive cop, however, and he was feared by blacks. They called him "Mr. Henry" and gave him a wide berth and a deferential greeting when passing him on the street.

Ironically, it was Henry Cook who came to my rescue when I ran into a serious problem concerning an article I had written—one that made headlines on sports pages throughout the country. It involved an exclusive story I wrote in 1949. That day Mr. Eisendrath, who obviously didn't know a thing about baseball, asked if I knew of a Stan Musial of St. Louis. I started reeling off statistics, telling him that the year before, "Stan the Man" had hit thirty-nine home runs and batted .387 and been named the National League's Most Valuable Player. I further informed him that Musial was the St. Louis Cardinals' superstar, right up there with Joe DiMaggio of the New York Yankees and Ted Williams of the Boston Red Sox.

Well, Mr. Eisendrath said, Louis Woods, the manager of the Hotel Biloxi, had called to say that Stan Musial, a baseball player from St. Louis, had checked into the hotel. If he was all that important, Mr. Eisendrath said, I should get a quick interview with him on the telephone since we were close to deadline.

The Hotel Biloxi, a grand old brick colonial building on the beach, was a favorite stop for VIPs. I had written stories about such well-known guests as General George C. Marshall and Mrs. Harry Truman and her daughter, Margaret. (When I tried to take a photograph of the First Lady with the *Herald*'s big Burke and James press camera, a Secret Service agent rushed up and made me move to the other side. "Mrs. Truman doesn't like to be photographed from that side," he brusquely informed me. I quickly switched sides and shot her photo; I was bursting with pride when the *Herald* played it on page one along with my story.)

Since there were no major league teams in the South in those days and St. Louis was in Missouri, a border state, Biloxians and many other southerners considered the Cardinals their home team. The chance to interview Musial was a once-in-a-lifetime opportunity for a nineteen-year-old sports-crazed reporter. I called Hotel Biloxi and asked for Stan Musial's room. When a man answered the phone I said, "Mr. Musial, this is Jack Nelson of the *Daily Herald*. Are you the Stan Musial of the St. Louis Cardinals?"

He said he was and explained that he and his wife had stopped in Biloxi for two days of relaxation before continuing to the Cardinals' spring training camp in Florida. Musial was considered a gentleman on and off the field and was never known for boasting. But in answer to a question, he told me he was shooting for the .400 batting mark that year. It was a hell of an interview and the *Herald* ran my story at the top of the sports page. The Associated Press picked it up and it ran in newspapers all over the country. Among other things, I wrote:

> The famous first baseman, who led National League swatters with a .387, says he has been practicing batting on his ranch in Texas and believes he will break the .400 mark.
>
> The Cardinal slugger also has high hopes of bettering his total of 39 homeruns in 1948. "I believe the batting practice I had on my ranch near El Paso has helped my distance, too," he said.
>
> Musial foresees not only a better season for himself, but also a better one for the St. Louis ball club as a whole. "It looks like we're going to have a darn good season," he said, adding that the Cardinals have acquired a number of good players from the Pacific Coast and Texas Leagues.

My words! Going out coast-to-coast! I could hardly contain my excitement, thinking my story must be the talk of millions of baseball fans. The story had prompted a flood of calls to the hotel, and news organizations from other towns and states were clamoring for interviews. The hotel sent a gift package to Musial's room, and a lunch was scheduled in his honor at the Biloxi Veterans Administration Center.

That evening I got a call from Mr. Eisendrath, who wanted to know if I was sure the person I interviewed on the phone was *the* Stan Musial. Of course it was, I said. I pointed out that he was registered as Stan Musial of St. Louis. He knew all of Musial's lifetime statistics. And he said he was on his way to spring training in Florida, which was what major league players were doing at that time. I was pretty indignant that anyone would doubt it was Musial.

Mr. Eisendrath said the question was raised by an AP reporter in New Orleans who said he didn't believe Musial owned a ranch in Texas. "What should I tell the AP?" Mr. Eisendrath asked.

"AP, they think they know everything," I said. "Tell 'em it was Stan Musial." He did and I went off to Gulfport for a meeting of the Naval Reserve unit I had recently joined.

Later that night after returning from Gulfport, I got another call from Mr. Eisendrath. AP had checked with Cardinal headquarters in St. Louis and located Musial in Albany, New York. "Better go down tomorrow and find out who it was you interviewed," Mr. Eisendrath said.

Crushed and humiliated, I hurried to the police station the next day and poured out the story to Chief Earl Wetzel and Henry Cook, who by now had been promoted to assistant chief. "Hell, Scoop," Wetzel said, "we can't do nothin' about that. There ain't no law says someone can't claim he's Stan Musial." Cook winked at me and said, "Let's go get a cup of coffee, Scoop."

Over coffee at the French Café, Cook said he figured anyone impersonating a famous baseball player like Musial probably had done something to break the law. We drove to Hotel Biloxi where Cook arranged with Louis Woods, the hotel manager, to eavesdrop on the imposter's telephone calls. Seeking a court order to do that was unheard of in those days.

The man I interviewed turned out to be a twenty-four-year-old drifter from Texas who had left a trail of bad checks from Los Angeles to Biloxi. The 1947 Chevrolet Fleetline he was driving had been bought in New Orleans with a bad check.

With Henry Cook's help I got two more exclusive stories—one on page one headlined, "Man Who Posed as Baseball Star Held in Biloxi" and another inside the paper headlined, "Fake Ball Player Admits He Cashed Seven Bad Checks."

For years after the Musial stories appeared, when I walked along Howard Avenue, Biloxi's main street, folks who knew me would call out, "Hey, Stan the Man."

The Musial episode was a tough but valuable learning experience for a rookie reporter. Never again would I be so cocksure of the identity of someone I had never met in person but was interviewing on the phone. A second tough learning experience happened several months later when I was covering federal court. I checked some records of a case in which a postal employee was sentenced to prison after pleading guilty to theft from the mail. Instead of using the employee's name as the defendant in the story I mistakenly used the name of his defense attorney.

To put it mildly, the attorney was not pleased and threatened to sue the *Herald*. The long-time owner and publisher, E. P. Wilkes, known as Mr. Gene, thought of it as a nuisance suit that the attorney could not win since he was identified in the story as a postal employee. But rather than risk the inconvenience and cost of a court trial, Wilkes bought him off for five hundred dollars, a substantial sum in those days. The publisher never said a word to me about the incident, but his silence was searing. I would never again make such careless assumptions without checking the facts.

Chapter 5

SIN AND SALT WATER

IN THE LATE 1940s, race relations were ignored by the *Daily Herald*, which for that matter was true of most other newspapers in the South. About the only time a black person's name appeared in the paper was when one was charged with a crime. As for me, I lacked any sensitivity on the subject and rarely gave the matter much thought, although I suppose I accepted separation of the races as a matter of course. Still, an experience I had a year or so after joining the paper jolted me. I was talking to a young desk clerk in the Biloxi police station when an elderly black man walked in. The clerk, not much older than I was, looked up and snapped, "Get that hat off your head, nigger!"

The black man quickly removed his hat, but the desk clerk's harsh tone shocked me. It was one of the first times I felt a tinge of shame about the system—not just segregation, but the notion of white supremacy. I found the clerk's comment repugnant—in part because, having been brought up to respect age, I was shocked that a young man could be so rude to an elderly person. And it was the first time I had heard "nigger" used in such a hostile way, although the word was routinely used by most white southerners when referring to blacks.

I said nothing to the clerk, however. Given the times and circumstances, I figured it was a no-win situation. On top of that, honesty compels me to admit, I knew that protesting the clerk's conduct could have cost me a source, a not inconsequential consideration at the time.

At the *Herald* my annual salary was $2,536.65, and I made a little extra money by freelancing for the *American Weekly* and New York's Universal Trade Press Syndicate. I loved reporting but finally decided I would be better off financially doing something else. That's when I applied for a clerical job with the FBI, hoping to eventually become an agent.

Like many young men in that era, I thought J. Edgar Hoover was one of the greatest living Americans. I saw FBI agents as heroes, their manly deeds portrayed in *The FBI in Peace and War*, a weekly radio program sponsored by Lava soap that I never missed. I had been encouraged to apply by Warren Toole, Biloxi's resident FBI agent, who said if I got the appointment I could go to college while working in Washington and could qualify as an agent after I graduated.

The FBI's file on me, which I received many years later under the Freedom of Information Act, was eye-opening. Although I was only applying for a clerical position, the bureau investigated me as thoroughly as if I had applied to be an undercover agent. Agents not only went back to Notre Dame High School to conduct interviews; they also investigated all the other schools I had attended in Alabama, Georgia, and Mississippi and talked with people in every town where I had lived. My name was run through the files of all U.S. intelligence agencies and the files of the House Un-American Activities Committee.

An agent interviewed me in person for almost an hour, and I guess I managed to impress him because he gave me a pretty positive review. "Nelson is an aggressive, energetic young man," he wrote. "He has a good personality and appears neatly dressed at all times. He is apparently an intelligent fellow who desires to further enhance his position in life. He is well above the average of usual clerical applicant prospects. Personal contact with him gives the impression that he is straightforward in his dealings, honest in his endeavors."

While waiting for word on my application, I got my first taste of investigative reporting. I began writing about the illegal gambling and liquor sales that flourished openly in Biloxi and along the Mississippi coast. Winking at state laws prohibiting gambling and liquor sales was seen as a Biloxi tradition. And with so many thousands of soldiers arriving at Keesler in the 1940s, Biloxi became a wide-open, anything-goes town. Gambling was so pervasive you could find slot machines and horse-race contraptions whirring in grocery and drug stores day and night. Nightclubs offered roulette wheels and blackjack tables. B-girls were numerous, prostitution rampant, and the venereal disease rate was so high that Keesler put some places off limits to soldiers.

I wrote one article after another in 1949 exposing the extent of the vice in Biloxi, tracing some of it to New Orleans and Carlos Marcello, the gambling kingpin of the Big Easy. He had been targeted by Senator Estes

Kefauver's Committee to Investigate Organized Crime, and the link to Biloxi eventually brought the city national publicity, not all of it welcome. It also put considerable heat on the *Herald.*

It's not as if Mr. Eisendrath or Mr. Wilkes encouraged me to write about the gambling and prostitution. But they didn't discourage me either, and I learned early on that if I wrote such stories they would have the courage to publish them. And it took courage because, in addition to incurring the wrath of racketeers, the articles infuriated legitimate businessmen who advertised in the *Daily Herald* and feared the articles would discourage tourism.

The Biloxi Chamber of Commerce had a combative bantam rooster of an executive director—Tony Ragusin—who bristled at every article. He would barge into the Biloxi newsroom demanding that Mr. Eisendrath stop publishing the stories. Mr. Eisendrath, soft-spoken but always firm, would chuckle and say, "Just calm down, my friend, calm down or you'll have a heart attack." Several times I witnessed these encounters and smiled to myself as Ragusin stormed out of the newsroom.

Mr. Eisendrath didn't like upsetting people, but he didn't seem to mind if I did. He once told me, "You'll do fine as a reporter because you don't mind making people mad." Actually, while I never enjoyed making people mad, like other journalists who specialize in investigative reporting, I learned that making people angry, sometimes dangerously so, comes with the territory.

Early in my investigations, one of the racketeers had the nerve to threaten me right outside the police station, in the presence of the police chief, Earl Wetzel, no less. "If you don't quit writin' about the slots," he snarled, "you gonna wind up in Back Bay with concrete for shoes."

Wetzel was a tall, muscular, blunt-spoken man. And, as Biloxians would put it, "He didn't' take nuthin' off nobody." He stuck his face right up to the racketeer's face, shook a thick finger under his nose, and said in a booming voice, "Anything happens to Scoop, you the first one I come lookin' for." The racketeer claimed he had just been joking, and I never heard anything else from him.

Yet the police themselves, and to some extent, the *Herald*, abetted the commercial vice. All the while the police were cooperating with me on gambling stories, they participated in a scheme shaking down illegal gambling and liquor operators for city revenue. And every month the *Herald* knowingly published a list of phony names of supposed gambling and liquor operators and the "fines" levied against them for illegal operations. (Pseudonyms had to be used because the third time a fine was levied, it would constitute a felony.)

Many years later Tony Creel, a city commissioner at the time whose job it was to enter the "fines" in city court documents, defended the practice as a way to keep city taxes low while supporting the police department. "Jack, we took in as much as a hundred thousand dollars a year and a hundred thousand dollars was a lot of money," he told me. "Earl Wetzel collected it and I recorded it. That supported our police department and fire department and our taxes were a lot lower then than they are now."

Because gambling affected so many people, my stories had the town in an uproar. Hundreds of people would cram into meetings called by a group of ministers who wanted to crack down on the slots. Tony Ragusin convened a meeting of businessmen at the Biloxi Community Center where he complained bitterly about me and the *Daily Herald* and declared that my articles were drying up the tourist trade. Some businesses that advertised in the *Herald* pressed the newspaper to stop publishing my articles on gambling, but Mr. Eisendrath and Mr. Wilkes, God bless them, never backed down.

Eventually, the *Saturday Evening Post* followed up on some of my stories and zeroed in on organized vice in Biloxi, running a long article entitled "Sin, Suds and Salt Water." Ragusin's worst fears were realized. A subcommittee of Senator Kefauver's committee held hearings on organized crime on the Mississippi coast. Stories about the hearings filled the front pages of the *Herald* for days and made for good reading. "Have you seen a slot machine reach out and grab a person to play it?" Tony Creel was quoted as saying. It was the first time I realized investigative reporting could have such dramatic impact. It was a shot of pure adrenalin for a young reporter.

In those days most newspapermen, especially in small towns, didn't worry too much about possible conflicts of interest. At the *Herald* such conflicts were everyday occurrences. I was in so tight with the police that they once used me as a decoy to help them find a man who had been beating up prostitutes. Outfitted in a tight skirt, sandals, and a wig, I walked along the beach, swinging my purse, until the man accosted me. The cops promptly arrested him and I went back to the *Herald* and wrote a story about the arrest.

Neither Mr. Eisendrath nor I saw anything wrong with getting enmeshed in the local community. Mr. Eisendrath was a member of the Lions Club and turned in stories about club meetings. And I became a member of the Rotary Club—a teen-age Rotarian!—and wrote about its doings.

Mr. Eisendrath may actually have been more involved in civic affairs than any other Biloxian. He was a member of just about every civic and fraternal group the *Herald* covered, including the chamber of commerce, the city planning committee, the Democratic Executive Committee, the Masonic Lodge, the USO Operating Committee, the Port Commission, the hospital board, the Red Cross chapter, and the local carnival organization.

Occasionally he would serve on a coroner's jury when one was empanelled to look into the cause of a death. Then he would write a story about the jury's findings. In fact, Mr. Eisendrath was a member of the coroner's jury that determined that the death of my father was accidental, and he later wrote an article about it under the headline "Howard Nelson Fatally Injured When Hit by Car." The article duly noted that Eisendrath was a member of the coroner's jury.

The coroner himself, "Tater" Hightower, had a pretty relaxed approach towards his duties. Often he would merely reach out and select a bystander when he needed to empanel a jury. Once I heard of a shooting death only blocks from the *Herald*'s office and rushed to the house to find the wife of a prominent elderly citizen running around shrieking, "Oh my God, I knew he was gonna do it, I knew he was gonna do it! I told him not to do it!"

Her husband lay sprawled in the backyard, the top of his head blown off and a shotgun at his feet. When Hightower arrived on the scene some time later he pointed to me and several others who were there and said he wanted us to serve on the coroner's jury to determine cause of death.

To me it was a clear case of suicide, both from the wife's shrieks and the fact that the top of the man's head was blown off even though his teeth were intact. Obviously, he had stuck the shotgun in his mouth and pulled the trigger. But the widow would collect double indemnity if it was an accident, and it soon became apparent that Hightower and other officials wanted a verdict of accidental death.

Witnesses were brought in to testify that it was hunting season and that the man probably was cleaning his shotgun when it accidentally went off. The other jurors agreed, but I protested, citing the evidence and what I had heard the victim's wife screaming. Hightower and the other jurors bore down on me, urging me to agree it was an accidental death. But I wouldn't budge. Hightower brought in the mayor, who testified it was hunting season, birds were flying overhead, and it was obvious the man had been cleaning his gun when it accidentally discharged. I thought that was outrageous and stood my ground.

Finally, Hightower looked at me and said, "How old are you, anyway?" "Twenty-one," I said with an air of triumph, knowing he was looking for a way to disqualify me. He went to the telephone and called my mother. She confirmed I had recently turned twenty-one.

That infuriated Hightower, and he returned and got together with the other jurors, all much older than I, and they started badgering me again. Finally, I caved and said, "Okay, have it your way, accidental." But I refused to write the story about the death and the jury's findings and vowed to myself I would never again succumb to such pressure if I was convinced I was right. It was Mr. Eisendrath who wrote up the jury's finding of "accidental death," making no mention of the debate over whether the death had been a suicide.

While I think I lived up to my promise to myself not to buckle under pressure, in those days I still cared a lot about what people thought. So I fretted when, after becoming a member of the Rotary Club board of directors, it came time for me to host a meeting of the board at our house. What worried me was the fact that we didn't have a coffee table. I had seen them at meetings held at other board members' houses. My mother was quite frugal and suggested we didn't really need a coffee table, but I rushed out and made a small down payment to buy one. I was afraid of being embarrassed when other board members saw how lacking we were in genteel furnishings.

Later I was feeling flush and made a down payment on my first car, a 1941 Chevrolet I proudly described as "forest green." And I was particularly proud that the steering wheel cover matched the car's seat covers, a fact that didn't seem to impress my mother or any of my friends nearly as much as it did me.

In September 1949, I finally received a letter from FBI headquarters signed by John Edgar Hoover, my idol, offering me a probationary appointment as an FBI clerk. The starting salary was "$2,284 per annum, less six per cent deduction for retirement purposes." The letter also noted that "before reporting for duty you should provide yourself with sufficient funds to enable you to live for at least one month before receiving your first salary check." The pay happened to be $252 a year less than I was making at the *Herald*. After deducting 6 percent for retirement I would be taking home $389 less.

I had second thoughts about joining the bureau, but it wasn't the pay that made me reconsider. By the time I received Hoover's letter, the impact of my investigative reporting had convinced me I would rather continue as a reporter. And I also had begun to realize that I was too independent and opinionated to be comfortable with the rigid discipline and regimentation Hoover demanded of his agents. So I wrote Hoover a letter thanking him for the appointment, but saying "circumstances have arisen since my application which will make it impossible for me to accept this appointment."

In view of all that was to follow in my relations with the FBI, my experience in applying for the clerkship and having my application accepted contains no small amount of irony: those FBI reports were the first entries in what over the years would become a voluminous dossier. The file included positive remarks on me when I was writing stories favorable to the FBI early in my career. But when I began writing stories exposing abuses and illegalities by Hoover and his FBI in the late sixties and early seventies, my dossier became filled with negative and exceptionally hostile memos and reports. The director went so far as to try to get my employer to fire me. But all that was much later. In the meantime, I was working day and night for the *Herald* and reveling in the action. But I wasn't too busy to notice a pretty girl who worked in the photo shop.

Out on the job, I lugged around the *Herald*'s big Burke and James press camera and frequently snapped photographs to accompany the stories. I always took the film to Lockett's Studio, about four blocks from the *Herald,* for developing and printing before the photos were delivered by car to the paper's publishing plant in Gulfport.

I wasn't much of a photographer and the striking young brunette who worked at the studio frequently teased me about the way I cut off the feet or the tops of the heads of my subjects. Her name was Virginia Dare Dickinson. I soon fell in love with her and she with me. But in 1951, our courtship was temporarily interrupted by my military service. The war in Korea was on.

Chapter 6

MY SO-CALLED MILITARY CAREER

I WAS NOT EAGER TO GO to the other side of the world to fight, so I joined the Mississippi National Guard along with my brother, Kenny, and my friend Al Rushing. I figured I could make a little extra money and perhaps stay out of Korea. We became members of Biloxi's Battery C of the 115th Anti-Aircraft Gun Battalion.

Because I was a reporter and could help with public relations and even write stories for the *Herald* about the National Guard, I was soon promoted to staff sergeant, a rank few of my colleagues ever attained. In fact my father never rose above corporal despite his meritorious service in World War II.

In May of 1951, with more reserves being called to duty because of extensive fighting in Korea, the 115th Battalion was federalized and ordered to Camp Stewart (now Fort Stewart), Georgia, then an anti-aircraft training center. The camp was huge, covering nearly three hundred thousand acres and extending into five counties—the largest military installation east of the Mississippi River. I immediately telephoned Lt. Albert Bacleda, the public information officer at Camp Stewart, and asked if he needed an assistant who had three and a half years of experience as a reporter.

Bacleda said he did, and after I arrived at Camp Stewart with Battery C, he arranged for me to be transferred to the camp headquarters unit and assigned to PIO as a public information supervisor. I had never undergone basic training or virtually any military training whatsoever. But I was good at what Bacleda thought was important—the ability to get my superiors' names and outfits in the paper.

Back in Biloxi the prime applicant for my job as a reporter at the *Herald* was Dick Lightsey, who booked horses and baseball games at the 20th Century Pool Hall, a favorite hangout for young Biloxians. Eisendrath hired him, but only after Lightsey agreed to cut his ties to the pool hall and its gambling operations. Years later Lightsey chuckled as he told me how Eisendrath wanted him to cover the Kefauver subcommittee's hearings on gambling. "I wouldn't do it," Lightsey said. "Hell, Jack, I thought they were gonna call me as a witness!"

During my so-called military service as a public information supervisor at Camp Stewart it quickly became clear that to get the camp and its commanding general publicity I needed to develop relations with the local news media. What better way to do it in those days than to work for the media? So that's what I did, moonlighting part-time for both the *Savannah Morning News*, about forty miles away, and the weekly *Liberty County Herald* in adjacent Hinesville, as well as occasionally writing for the *Atlanta Constitution*.

I also realized that in order to persuade the local media to publish positive news, it helped to play it straight when the news was negative. So, following a policy that most public relations professionals would probably consider laughable, or at the very least counterproductive, I never held back on negative incidents, going so far as to supply editors with detailed reports. When a soldier walked into the main post exchange and shot his wife to death, then shot himself, I quickly alerted an editor at the *Savannah Morning News*. Within a couple of hours, I telephoned the editor the full story of what happened.

And when Col. Lloyd A. Corchran, then the acting post commander, was shot to death while hunting turkeys on the Camp Stewart reservation, I quickly got the news out to the *Morning News* and the *Constitution*. After Drew Pearson reported in a radio broadcast that Corchran had been murdered, I quickly put out the word that an investigation showed that the colonel had been accidentally shot to death while crouched behind some bushes and sounding a turkey yelper. Later, I informed the media that a hunting companion, a chief warrant officer on the base and a survivor of the Bataan Death March in World War II, had confessed to investigators that he had mistaken Corchran for a turkey and shot him.

My military superiors supported my information policy of providing good and bad news because they saw that it paid off. And newspaper editors were so pleased to get such unaccustomed cooperation from the military that they returned the favor. News releases about events such as Armed Forces Day programs and stories featuring the exploits of Brigadier General Clare H. Armstrong, Camp Stewart's commanding general, always got good play in the local press.

General Armstrong was pleased, of course, especially since our news releases routinely opened by saying, "Brigadier Gen. Clare H. Armstrong, commanding general of Camp Stewart, Georgia, and Savior of Antwerp, Belgium, from German V-Bomb attacks during World War II, said today . . ." Generating that kind of publicity ingratiated me with my superiors and made it a lot less likely I would be subjected to the dreaded orders to FECOM, an acronym for Far East Command. The Savior of Antwerp, Belgium, obviously would not like to be deprived of the services of his chief publicist.

I was seeing Virginia whenever I got a chance, and not long after arriving at Camp Stewart she and I were married by a Catholic chaplain in a military ceremony at a camp chapel. Her parents didn't attend. They disapproved of the match because I was Catholic, and they were strict Baptists. But that didn't matter to a couple of happy newlyweds. We moved into a small apartment in Hinesville with a bathroom so tiny you had to sit sideways on the commode. Virginia made the best of it, but it couldn't have been easy for her. While I was out, making a name for myself, meeting all kinds of new and interesting people, she was stuck in a place where she hardly knew a soul. The apartment grew even more crowded when our first child, a beautiful daughter we named Karen, was born in July 1952.

Cramped or not, our apartment was a lot more comfortable than the quarters occupied by my colleagues in Biloxi's Battery C. They slept in tents. And while they were going through grinding military training I was happily turning out press releases in the relative comfort of an office at camp headquarters.

My brother, Kenny, and Al Rushing ribbed me about the relatively cushy life I was living while they endured rigorous training. But some of my other Battery C buddies were not amused, especially since I had a tendency to rub their noses in it. Was I insufferable? I guess I was.

Supplied with a car and driver when out on assignment, I'd sometimes see the Biloxians carrying rifles and heavy backpacks, marching off on a long, grueling hike. I'd have the driver pull over and as they passed by say, "Hi, guys, how's the training going?" "Goof-off" and "Fuck-up," they'd yell back, in tones that were far from friendly.

With the heavy schedule I was keeping, my days in the military seemed to pass fast. In addition to my public information work and moonlighting for several newspapers, I wrote a column, "Service Sports Slants," for *The Rocket*, the camp newspaper.

In December 1952, nineteen months after arriving at Stewart, I was scheduled to be discharged, yet I had never been through any training. That didn't go unnoticed at headquarters, where officers were astounded to find in their discharge pipeline a staff sergeant with no record of military training whatsoever. I was at my desk when the telephone rang. It was Master Sergeant Mayo from camp headquarters.

"Goddamit, Sergeant Nelson," he bellowed. "We gettin' ready to discharge you and you ain't even been through the infiltration course. You ain't even qualified for the .30 caliber carbine. Get yore ass down here so we can qualify you with the carbine and put yore ass through the infiltration course."

So I got my ass down there and in no time at all they qualified me for firing the .30 caliber carbine. I'm not sure my actual firing on the range met official standards, but they recorded me as qualified in a day. The next day they sent me through the infiltration course where you had to crawl on your belly with machine guns firing live ammunition only a few feet over your head. I knew all about the dangers of standing up because I had written news releases about other soldiers whose backsides were shot off when they raised up. So I slithered like a snake and somehow managed to make it through the infiltration course. After two days of military training, Sergeant Mayo recorded me as having been fully qualified for an honorable discharge.

Once out of service, I anguished over my next move. Cosman Eisendrath had written me a letter saying I could return as a reporter any time I wanted, and I had carried it around in my pocket and had been keen to accept the offer. But thanks to my occasional work for the *Constitution*, the managing editor, Bill Fields, also offered me a job. I loved Biloxi and the *Herald* and admired Mr. Eisendrath, who tutored me when I knew nothing about reporting and stood behind me when I goofed up. But the *Constitution* offer was tempting, not just because it offered a chance to move up to a much larger paper and the possibility of going to college under the G.I. Bill. It was the big time, and by 1953, I felt ready.

Chapter 7

ATLANTA

FOR AN AMBITIOUS REPORTER LIKE ME, going to work for the *Constitution* seemed like a good fit, but I wanted certain assurances first. I flew to Atlanta to discuss the offer with Bill Fields, and told him I was willing to work long hours but that I also wanted to go to college. He said he understood but expressed doubts that my going to college would work well for the *Constitution*.

"We'll pay you eighty-five dollars a week if you don't go to college because you'll be available to us, if needed, twenty-four hours a day," he said. "But we'll pay you seventy-five dollars if you do go to college because we won't be able to call on you when you're in classes." I decided to take the seventy-five dollars and go to college. I enrolled at the Atlanta Division of the University of Georgia, a downtown institution with class-rooms then located in a huge renovated garage. Its students were mostly young adults who worked full time and attended classes either at night or during the day, including many like me attending under the G.I. Bill, the only way most of us could afford it.

In an unheard-of burst of generosity, Fields decided to pay me eighty-five dollars a week anyway, which, he gave me to understand, was a major concession on the part of the paper. Stories about penny-pinching at the *Journal* and *Constitution* in those days were legion, and Fields in particu-lar was known as a tightwad. A wiry, balding ex-marine who had no use for small talk and seldom smiled, he saw eye to eye with the publisher, Jack Tarver, who was so tight-fisted we used to joke that he sat in his office squeezing nickels until they turned into dimes.

Reporters assigned to stories in the downtown area were supplied with bus tokens. No taxis for us. Once when I asked for an advance to cover a story in Milledgeville, seventy miles south of Atlanta, Fields authorized twenty-five dollars. I was incredulous and laughingly asked if he thought

I was going to the nearby suburb of Marietta. He didn't laugh. He didn't authorize any extra money either. Pay raises were pitiful—five or ten dollars a week at the most—and rare. But Fields's decision to pay me eighty-five dollars a week was a godsend because now that I had started a family, I badly needed the money.

In spite of its penurious ways, the *Constitution* was an invigorating place to work in those days. We competed fiercely for scoops with the *Atlanta Journal*, the afternoon paper, even though both papers had the same owner: former Ohio governor James M. Cox. My archrival at the *Journal* was John Pennington, who was one hell of a reporter, and I was obsessed with beating him. I was constantly nosing around, trying to find out what he was working on, determined to get there before he did.

The *Constitution* staff of about thirty reporters and editors was close-knit and populated by an assortment of colorful characters, some of them brilliant. One of my favorites was Celestine Sibley, a big-boned, warm-hearted country girl who wrote like a dream, even though her personal life was full of tragedy. She was the original sob sister. She'd write the kind of stories that would bring tears to your eyes, then turn around and produce a razor-sharp article on the state legislature. Lee Fuhrman, an old night rewrite man who sipped from a bottle he barely bothered to conceal in his desk, would regale us with stories about the Lindbergh trial and assorted lurid murders he had covered back in Philadelphia. Then there was Eddie Barker, another great storyteller and phrasemaker who liked a nip or two. Once he was assigned to cover a Jaycees convention at a hotel in downtown Atlanta, and after availing himself of the open bar, he came back and wrote that the Jaycees were just a "bunch of mice training to be rats." (If I remember correctly, his story was pulled after the first edition.)

The biggest laugh we ever had made the paper look a little silly. I was still a very junior reporter working nights when three guys walked into the newsroom carrying a two-foot hairless creature of some kind. They told us they had been driving around in a truck in rural Cobb County when they saw what looked like a spaceship in the road and three small space aliens walking around. Two of the creatures hopped back on their craft and zoomed away, but the men claimed they accidentally ran over the third. We thought the tale was pretty far-fetched, but the night editor called in a veterinarian who examined the critter and said, "I don't know what it is, but it's not of this earth." Somebody—I don't remember who—wrote a tongue-in-cheek story which ran on page one the next day, complete with a staff photo. This was in 1953, when the UFO craze was at its zenith, so the story was picked up all over the world, causing phones in the newsroom to ring nonstop. The Georgia Bureau of Investigation took a more skeptical view and interrogated the men—two barbers and a butcher—at length. They finally broke down and confessed to what ever after would be known as the Great Monkey Hoax. One of the barbers had bet others that he could get his picture in the paper. So they got hold of a monkey which he shaved and chloroformed. The butcher then killed it before lopping off its tail. It made for quite a correction the following day. (I'm told the GBI still has the beast in formaldehyde somewhere.)

Atlanta itself was exciting in those days—a bustling city expanding outwards in all directions, far more cosmopolitan than Georgia as a whole. The city fathers had begun courting northern investment as early as the twenties, promoting Atlanta as a business-friendly center of manufacturing, transportation, and banking. Although segregation was rigidly enforced until the sixties, the town had a reputation for racial moderation, which helped attract businesses and out-of-town conventions. William Hartsfield, who served six terms as mayor and owed his longevity to the black vote, dubbed Atlanta "the city too busy to hate."

The rest of Georgia, still heavily agrarian, regarded Atlanta as an outpost of Gomorrah. Jimmy Carter once said that when he was growing up in Plains, making a trip to Atlanta was like going to Moscow or Beijing. But Atlanta was proud of its reputation as the capital of the New South, and hometown boosterism was the order of the day. The Atlanta papers, members in good standing of the establishment, joined in with editorials extolling the city's attractions. Not that the *Constitution* and the *Journal* marched to the same beat editorially. The *Journal*'s editorial page tended to be conservative, while the *Constitution*'s was liberal— an arrangement the publisher evidently adopted because he thought it made business sense.

When I first got there, the *Journal* had the larger circulation—roughly 275,000 readers to the *Constitution*'s 200,000. But as the fifties progressed, the *Journal*, like most other afternoon papers, steadily lost readers to television news. (The *Constitution* finally surpassed the *Journal* in the seventies.) But even when it was the smaller of the two, the *Constitution* had more prestige, mainly because it had Ralph McGill. He was already a towering figure in American journalism, a man whose moral force was equaled only by the eloquence of his writing. His column, which ran on the front page of the paper seven days a week, frequently on the theme of racial justice, was must reading, even for those who hated him. A few years later, when Eugene Patterson, another brilliant writer and commanding presence, joined the editorial staff, publisher Jack Tarver likened the duo—accurately, to my way of thinking—to Babe Ruth and Lou Gehrig.

The paper, which was distributed statewide, wielded enormous clout in Georgia, especially in the realm of politics. I used to see politicians of all stripes—the mayor, city aldermen, state legislators—drop by the editorial offices just to chat. On election night, the *Constitution* newsroom was election central. Everyone—radio, TV, the candidates—came to our newsroom because we had the most complete information, including at least one reliable person assigned to almost every county. Their job was to give us the returns before they could be altered and the election stolen—a not uncommon event in Georgia. Outside, the returns would be projected on the side of the building, always drawing a good-sized crowd.

McGill himself could alter the outcome of an election. He is generally credited with installing Ellis Arnall, a relative moderate, as governor in 1942, ousting the notorious race-baiter Gene Talmadge. (Talmadge, not surprisingly, loathed McGill. One of his flunkies once threatened to kill the editor.)

McGill, who won a Pulitzer Prize for his columns on civil rights in 1959, had a great sense of moral outrage, especially at the injustices inflicted on minorities and other disadvantaged people. I was tremendously proud to be associated with him. Often described as the "conscience of the South," he was constantly being quoted in *Time* magazine, the *New York Times*, and other national publications. Probably no other major newspaper in the country was so intimately identified with its star columnist.

Being known as one of McGill's reporters could be good or bad, depending upon where you were and whom you were talking to. Outside of the South, his name was magic. In 1961–62 when I attended Harvard University on a Nieman Fellowship, just mentioning that I worked for Ralph McGill's paper opened doors for me. It was often the opposite in the South, where many considered him a traitor to the region.

While McGill truly loved the South and often wrote poetically of its beauty, he mostly focused on the region's faults. He wrote about the cruelty and brutality of Jim Crow laws. He stressed such things as the fact that the South's rate of rejections for selective service was 50 percent higher than the national average—and the fact that the high rejection rate came from the South's educational deficiencies and its high rates of mental illness and venereal disease.

"No thoughtful citizen would wish to cover up such a record," he wrote. "He would insist something be done about it. We have not done a good job. Whatever the reasons, and some of them are valid, we can't fail to work on this record."

Such columns enraged not only members of the Ku Klux Klan and other hate groups. His critics included many of the region's leaders in politics, labor, business and the professions—even journalism and religion. To these detractors, he replied in a column that he agreed with Marse Henry Watterson, the famed Louisville editor, who once declared:

Things have come to a hell of a pass
When a man can't flog his own jackass.

As to the accusations of disloyalty, McGill wrote: "Who loves his region more—he who fights those things in it which are ugly and wrong and unjust or he who says, 'Let us dwell on our lovely sunsets and our beautiful fields and not advertise our faults'?"

Although McGill became a national figure for his courageous, often lonely stand against segregation, it's worth noting that his stance evolved gradually. In the 1940s, he was a moderate, at least by southern standards; he called for justice for the Negro while defending segregation, saying integration was "not desirable from the viewpoint of either race."

Gradually, he took a more forceful line against segregation, always conscious of not getting too far ahead of his audience. Once the Supreme Court ruled against segregated schools in 1954, however, he urged the South to accept the ruling as the law of the land and forthrightly denounced racism in all its forms. (In this respect, he was far ahead of me. I was still turning my eyes away from the subject.)

With violence never very far from the surface in those days, his columns provoked vicious reactions from racist whites. They shot buckshot through his windows, dumped garbage on his lawn, and called him "Rastus" and "Red Ralph." (McGill, who had a great sense of humor, named his schnauzer Rastus, and sometimes when he got hate calls at home asking for Rastus, he'd say, "Wait a minute. I'll call him.")

Like everyone else, I was in awe of the man. A stocky, rumpled figure with black hair and a gravelly voice, he was adored by people who were close to him. His deputy, Gene Patterson, called him Pappy and thought he was a saint. But to us reporters, he seemed a somewhat distant figure, too wrapped up in national and international issues to be very interested in our work. He did not appear in the newsroom very often. He traveled a lot, and when he was in town he wrote his columns in a large office just down the hall.

At the same time, McGill was intensely loyal to his friends, and he became keenly and personally interested in a couple of investigative stories I worked on when they involved friends of his. One of the investigations centered on a police-protected lottery ring in Atlanta and resulted in the first of two unpleasant encounters I would have with him about stories I was writing.

The first run-in was especially painful for me, because I had invested so much time in unearthing the facts surrounding the lottery ring, and the story was so big and explosive: the lottery operation took in close to two million dollars a year and involved extensive police corruption. But first I had to find out where the ring operated. I'd been trying, without success, to chip away at the story for two years when, in 1957, I got my first real break. I heard that an Atlanta policeman had been shifted off his beat after reporting on the existence of a lottery ring. I started pounding his old beat, asking residents and store owners if they knew anything at all. Finally a woman pointed me to the auto repair garage next door, owned by a man named Horace Ingram, where she said there was a lot of coming and going but not much in the way of auto repairing. I began working closely with a federal agent—something which wouldn't happen today—and the woman let us watch what was going on from her upstairs kitchen window. I sat up there for eleven days, just ten feet from the asphalt apron of the garage, watching as two police cars with their numbers clearly painted on their front doors stopped by the garage nearly every day. Using binoculars, I could also see Ingram, the lottery operator, handing money to the officers. At one point, I was joined by Tom McRae, the assistant managing editor, who took moving pictures of the transactions which were later used in the trial

We had a couple of dicey moments. Once McRae was taking slow motion footage, and the whirring of the camera was so loud I was sure we'd be discovered. Another time, a couple of mobsters seemed to be staring directly up at the window. We never were discovered, though, and the *Constitution* splashed my story and McRae's photos across page one. That was gratifying, but the stories and photos clearly upset McGill and his close friend, Mayor William Hartsfield, both of whom took great pride in the Atlanta police.

Hartsfield was especially upset about the story because he was coming up for reelection. He came storming into the newsroom, saying, "After the election, there's going to be some changes around here." But there never were, of course. As colorful and profane as he was canny, Hartsfield had a talent for alliteration, especially when it came to cursing. He referred to Bill Fields as "a beady-eyed bastard" and called *Journal* editor Jack Spaulding a "supercilious shit-ass."

Hartsfield's friend Ralph McGill was not happy about our disclosures either. Although he seldom voiced opinions about the news side, when McGill heard we were planning to run the police-protected lottery story, he dropped by my desk and asked me whether we had "the deadwood" on the police.

"Oh yeah, we got the deadwood, no doubt about that," I assured him.

McGill shrugged and went back to his office and wrote a lead editorial that downplayed the seriousness of the lottery investigation, declaring that "a few rotten apples don't spoil the barrel."

I was only twenty-eight years old and was dealing with a Great Man who was older and who was my superior. But I was upset because it seemed to me he wasn't facing facts. I thought he'd been blinded by his friendship with Hartsfield and his pride in the Atlanta police, whose popular and highly regarded chief, Herschel Jenkins, was also a friend of McGill's. I didn't say anything to McGill, but in the newsroom I had a lot to say about my displeasure, which I'm sure got back to him. However, he never brought it up with me again.

My exposé did not exactly have the expected impact. Some of the racketeers were found guilty of bribing the policemen, but the policemen were all acquitted of accepting bribes. That was bad enough in my view, but I also had to contend with some serious harassment from angry police and their supporters. People would call up and say, "How are you and your family doing? I hope you are going to have a merry Christmas, because there are policemen and their families who aren't because of you." The police in DeKalb County, the suburb where I lived, joined in the vendetta. Several times late at night, I would hear a commotion and look out the window to find cops coming towards the house with their flashlights in one hand and their pistols in the other, claiming they had received reports that I had killed my wife. Other times, fire trucks roared up with sirens screaming. It was frightening, and obviously upset Virginia, although she accepted it as part of the job, the same way a policeman's or fireman's wife would.

My next unpleasant encounter with McGill occurred a couple of years later. I was spending my vacation time at home—we couldn't afford to go anywhere on my salary—when I got a call from a teacher at a small college. He was a member of a state committee that had been appointed to look into whether Massey Business College was qualified to be designated a state college. Massey was run by Anna Lee Porter, a glamorous blonde who was a good friend of McGill's.

The college teacher offered to give me a copy of his committee's report, which was critical of Massey Business College in several respects and recommended that Massey not be granted state college status. The teacher was incensed because the state department of education had overruled the committee and given Massey the designation anyway.

After getting the report, I came in off vacation to try to develop a story. I found that Reg Murphy, the paper's political reporter, was working on a similar story about Massey, though without a copy of the report, so we agreed to work together.

At the state department of education, I asked Claude Purcell, the state school superintendant, why Massey had gotten state college status despite the committee's recommendation. The main reason, he said, was that a number of highly regarded people had sent letters strongly recommending the status be conferred despite the committee's findings.

"Who are these folks?" I asked. "I'd like to see copies of their letters."

"Well, there's one of the letters you probably don't want to see," Purcell said, "because if you see it, you probably won't want to write a story." Of course, he couldn't have said anything that would have done more to whet my appetite. "That's the one letter I do want to see," I told him.

He pulled out a file of letters, riffled through it, then handed me a letter from Ralph McGill finding fault with the committee's report and strongly recommending Massey for state college status. Purcell gave me a copy of the letter.

At the *Constitution*, I found McGill none too pleased to be questioned about his letter and the committee's findings. He spoke tersely, saying only that he considered Massey to be an excellent institution and that he thought the committee's report was unfair.

The story I wrote with Reg Murphy was played big on Page One and created a substantial hubbub in political and higher education circles, not to mention in the *Constitution* newsroom. It also resulted in a tirade of memos—we called them pink memos because they were typed on pink paper—from McGill to the managing editor and city editor, criticizing me and Murphy. McGill sent both me and Murphy copies of his memos.

I no longer have copies, but some of the language was so strong it's burned in my memory. In the first one McGill said that story we had written was one of the worst he had ever seen and that I made him "ashamed of the paper." He went on to say what a great service Massey performed in providing education for folks who might otherwise not attend college.

I had gone back home to resume my vacation when McGill's memos were circulated. Howell Jones, the city editor, telephoned me and read me the text and asked if I wanted to reply to it. I told him no, that it was just McGill reacting that way because he was such a close friend of Anna Lee Porter. I added that I thought his memo was both so over the top and so off the mark I didn't see any need to reply to it.

The next day I got another call from Howell Jones, who said McGill had sent us all a second memo, this one even more blistering than the first. McGill wrote that in retrospect, the Massey article was "one of the worst hatchet jobs and pieces of yellow journalism I've ever seen." The memo went on at some length in that harsh vein.

I found it infuriating. Here I had produced what I considered to be a solid story based on all the evidence, and McGill had trashed the story and impugned my integrity. This time, I told Jones, I would write a reply. Reg, who said he was just as angry and felt as unfairly criticized as I, said he too would write a reply.

Like McGill, I addressed my memo to the managing editor and city editor, with a copy to McGill. I began by saying that McGill had unfairly accused me of "yellow journalism" and that he owed me an apology, but that judging from the tone of his memos, I didn't expect one. Then I carefully laid out the facts of how in response to a college professor's call, I, along with Murphy, had thoroughly researched the story, including getting McGill's side of his part in it, before turning the story over to the city desk. I wrote that I was proud of the story and stood behind it as accurate.

Murphy also wrote a memo, beginning at some length with what great respect he had for McGill, which I, in my outraged state, thought was unnecessary and beside the point, especially in light of McGill's second memo. (Murphy rose to become the editor of the *Atlanta*

Constitution, going on to hold the top posts at the *San Francisco Examiner*, the *Baltimore Sun*, and the *National Geographic*.

In any event, in reply to our memos, McGill wrote a third one that began something like this: "After receiving a polite but firm memo from Reg Murphy and an angry memo from Jack Nelson, I understand there is some feeling they consider my memos were too harsh . . ." Then, without ever really apologizing for his unwarranted accusations, he went on to reiterate at some length his belief that our story unfairly criticized the awarding of state college status to Massey. I never heard another word from McGill about the matter.

Later, after I went to work for the *Los Angeles Times* and was covering civil rights out of Atlanta, I got to know McGill better, and we became friends. He used to invite me, Gene Roberts, and other national reporters based in Atlanta up to his office to brief him on what we'd been hearing and seeing out in the field. And while we never became intimates, I respected and admired him greatly, especially for his courageous, sensitive writing and strong stands on civil rights and other issues of fairness. I consider him one of the great American editors of the twentieth century.

I'm ashamed to admit I didn't always read McGill's column while I worked for the *Constitution*. I was not writing about racial problems and was not especially sensitive to them at the time. The *Constitution*'s power structure was equally indifferent. The battle for racial justice that McGill waged in his column and on the editorial pages generally got little or no support from the rest of the paper.

As editor, McGill ran the editorial pages, but he had no authority and relatively little influence over what the news side covered—not even later after he was promoted to publisher. News remained the domain of the dour managing editor Bill Fields, who was all-powerful in the newsroom. And the *Constitution*'s lawyers and business executives—in part out of concern about libel suits stemming from McGill's fiery columns—counseled the managing editor to be restrained in covering civil rights. Fields, who had little use for the civil rights movement and worried that it had been infiltrated by communists, was happy to oblige.

McGill's successor, Gene Patterson, who also won a Pulitzer Prize for editorials attacking racism, did not have much influence over news coverage either. As a result, the *Constitution*'s coverage of the civil rights movement, except for minimal reporting of state and local developments, consisted primarily of wire service stories that not only were relatively superficial but were usually heavily edited. *Constitution* reporters seldom wrote about the overall movement, even when it was the biggest story in the country and despite the fact that Atlanta was the home of Dr. Martin Luther King Jr. and that Daddy King, his father, still preached every Sunday from the pulpit of Ebenezer Baptist Church.

For my part, I was covering corruption in government, staying away from civil rights stories except in rare cases. In part, this was a deliberate decision. Fields reasoned that my getting involved would alienate sources, especially in the field of law enforcement, and would hamper my investigations. I could see the wisdom in this and went along with him. Later, when I became deeply involved in covering civil rights, I would look back with great regret over the opportunities I had missed in covering the early years of what was, in my opinion, the greatest story of the twentieth century.

Chapter 8

BACK ON THE VICE BEAT

A FEW MONTHS after joining the *Constitution* in 1953, I got an urgent telephone call that sent me off on a major investigation and one of my most harrowing experiences as a reporter. Brigadier General Richard Mayo, who had succeeded General Armstrong as commander of Camp Stewart, told me that gambling, drinking, and prostitution, under the protection of Liberty County officials, were victimizing soldiers and seriously hampering their training for combat duty in Korea.

Most of the soldiers were young inductees who were lonely and easily led astray. Teenaged barmaids, many from out of town, were luring the trainees into gambling joints and fleecing them of their money. And prostitutes were beckoning them into whorehouses where they were contracting venereal diseases at an alarming rate. The general, fiercely protective of his troops' welfare and morale, expressed outrage that soldiers were out gambling, drinking, and whoring around until well after midnight and then having to get up at 4:30 a.m. to be on the firing range at 6 a.m. He was concerned they would not be properly trained when they shipped out to Korea.

Mayo said he had spoken to local authorities about the problems to no avail and asked that I investigate and expose the corruption. From my time at Camp Stewart I knew that Hinesville and Liberty County were rough-and-tumble places where a courthouse gang headed by Sheriff Paul Sikes and his brother-in-law, Judge Paul Caswell, ruled with an iron hand. But I told the general I would do what I could.

It was no secret that slot machines and other forms of gambling operated illegally outside Camp Stewart. In fact, when we were based there some of my colleagues from Battery C patronized the gambling joints, although I never heard of anyone being victimized. In fact, they had so much practice skimming horse racing machines in Biloxi, they were more like the victimizers than the victims. My buddies had developed a scheme that rigged the machines to pay off. Once the machine registered a winning horse they would jam a wire into the machine so the same choice would be registered as a winner on subsequent replays. For weeks they drained money from the machines until they were finally caught and barred from the gambling joints.

But while I already knew something about Liberty County politics and the gambling, I didn't know much about the prostitution, the high incidence of VD, and the way officials colluded to protect the vice establishments. Mayo's call was also the first I had heard of the military's concern that soldiers' training was being undermined by the vice raging there.

I returned to the Camp Stewart area with gusto, surveying the scene in detail and interviewing numerous soldiers and others who had intimate knowledge of both the gambling and prostitution. Soldiers were losing their paychecks in gambling joints situated so close to the camp that you could stand next to one of them and touch it with one hand while touching the fence surrounding the camp with the other hand.

There were gambling machines of various types in almost every establishment in Hinesville, including a dozen stores on the courthouse square in the center of downtown. Scantily clad girls, some obviously minors, plied the soldiers with drinks as they gambled, and in some cases sold them sexual favors after closing. I wrote about the extraordinarily high venereal disease rate at Stewart and about the whorehouses that lured them inside, including one house that turned out to be operated by a deputy sheriff.

The VD rate for Camp Stewart had soared to 42.8 in the month before I visited Liberty County, which, as Mayo pointed out, meant that if the rate continued for the next year, there would be 428 cases of VD for every 1,000 troops at Camp Stewart. My stories touched off a firestorm, and a Liberty County grand jury was quickly empanelled to investigate. After three days of testimony, during which several witnesses from Camp Stewart were put under military police protection because of threats, word that indictments were about to come down spread throughout the county. As night fell the jury returned forty-three indictments and charged Sheriff Sikes of knowingly failing and neglecting to enforce state liquor laws, a charge that could result in his ouster.

A crowd of forty or fifty people—some who had been indicted and others who were friends or relatives of those who had been indicted—milled around the courthouse lawn. Among them was Deputy Sheriff E. E. Dykes. I did not know the deputy's name at the time, but he was indicted for operating a gambling joint. He also operated a tourist court that had been placed off limits by Camp Stewart as a house of prostitution. Dykes's nickname was "Slim," but he was anything but. He was close to six feet, four inches tall and weighed about 220 pounds.

I was standing at the edge of the courthouse lawn, feeling rather proud about the grand jury's investigation and the indictments my stories had spurred when suddenly I saw a hulking figure approaching me. It was the deputy sheriff, cursing and clenching his fists as he barreled toward me, rasping, "You no good little son of a bitch." He grabbed me by the throat and spread-eagled me over the hood of a car in front of the courthouse. I struggled to get away, afraid he was going to choke me to death. I finally managed to break away and ran toward the courthouse.

Several people pushed me and I heard people murmuring things like "the little bastard got what he deserved" and "they ought to kill the son of a bitch." I made my way through the crowd to the foot of the courthouse steps where a Hinesville policeman I knew as David Carter was standing. I asked him to arrest the man on an assault and battery charge.

Carter, who obviously knew the man's name and had seen him attack me, said I'd have to know the man's name and swear out a warrant before he could arrest him. I turned to the attacker, who had followed me through the crowd and was standing nearby grinning, and said, "What's your name?" "Bill Jones," he said, obviously giving me a phony name, and grabbed me again. While others yelled, "Kill the little son of a bitch," Carter pulled him away from me, grabbed me by the arm, and escorted me into the courthouse.

We walked into the chambers of Judge Caswell, the sheriff's brother-in-law, and the judge was sitting stone-faced behind his desk. "This guy wants to swear out a warrant for assault and battery, says he got attacked outside the courthouse," Carter said.

Caswell didn't try to conceal his contempt. He pulled a warrant out of a desk drawer and in a sneering way asked, "What's the name of the man you say attacked you?"

"I don't know," I said, "But he attacked me in front of Officer Carter and about fifty other people. Officer Carter must know his name." Carter said nothing.

The judge said, "You don't know his name, you can't swear out a warrant," and he held the warrant over his head and crumpled it, letting it fall to the floor. Now I was really scared and walked quickly out of his office closely followed by Carter.

As I started down the courthouse steps the crowd became boisterous again with people yelling that they'd like a crack at me. My clothes
and rental car were still at the Hinesville hotel where I had been staying
during the grand jury investigation, but I didn't worry about that. I just
wanted to get out of town as quickly as possible.

I told Carter I was afraid for my life and that if he didn't protect me,
the FBI would hold him personally responsible. He grabbed me by the
arm and said, "Come on, let's go." He led me through the crowd to a
police car, shoved me in the back seat, then got in and drove off at a high
speed to Camp Stewart. There, the provost marshal put me into protective custody of the military police.

Military officials had monitored the courthouse confrontation, and it
had been so ugly and lasted so long that they alerted Georgia Governor Herman Talmadge that I was being endangered by a mob in Hinesville. Talmadge later told *Constitution* editors he had considered calling
out the National Guard until learning a Hinesville policeman had safely
escorted me from the scene to Camp Stewart.

At Camp Stewart the military police learned that Deputy Dykes and
R. V. Sikes, son of the sheriff, had sworn out a warrant charging me with
"disorderly conduct." Liberty County officials were demanding that I be
returned to Hinesville to be arrested. Although I wasn't eager to return
to Hinesville, Bill Fields, in a telephone conversation from Atlanta, said it
would not look good for me or the *Constitution* if I avoided arrest.

I agreed to return to Hinesville, but Camp Stewart officials were still
so concerned about my safety that they had the governor's office arrange
for a prominent local citizen, Major General Joseph B. Frazier of the
Georgia National Guard, to guarantee my safety. Military police escorted
me to the camp gate at Hinesville and Frazier was there to meet me. He
had arranged to sign my bond at the gate so I wouldn't have to go into
Hinesville where people were still milling around the courthouse lawn.
After he signed my bond, MPs escorted me back to safe quarters in Camp
Stewart.

Later, when I attended some of the trials that resulted from the indictments, a witness for the defendants, a B-girl from one of the gambling
joints, testified that I had tried to rape her during my investigations. The
charge was outlandish, of course, and I never faced any such criminal
charge. And the "disorderly conduct" count brought by Dykes and the
sheriff's son was dismissed. But the episode had been one of the closest
calls in my career.

Chapter 9

LITTLE ROCK

AS THE *CONSTITUTION*'S investigative reporter, a role I carved out for myself at a time when there were few investigative reporters anywhere in the South, I became well known as a muckraker throughout Georgia in the 1950s and early 1960s. In those days, muckraking was still looked down on in many quarters after flourishing briefly at the turn of the century, in the Progressive era. (It was Theodore Roosevelt who first applied the term to the press, quoting a line from *The Pilgrim's Progress* about a man with a muckrake in his hand who rejected salvation to concentrate on filth.)

Despite such criticism, my enthusiasm for muckraking or, if you prefer, investigative reporting, has never wavered. I still think it's the greatest service a free press can perform and—I hope this doesn't sound pompous—I believe it is indispensable to the well-being of society. While others may shy away from it, I was in my element, perhaps because of some quirks in my nature. Where the average person sees grey, I tend to see black and white. Not being terribly introspective may help too. My stories would often cause anguish to others, but it's not in my nature to dwell on the consequences. I focus all of my attention on the job I think needs to be done and leave the hand-wringing to others. I also have a low tolerance for official malfeasance. It's been said of me, and I guess it's true, that I get personally offended by wrongdoing. In my view, the police and government officials are supposed to do the right thing, and whenever I've found them engaging in shenanigans, I've never hesitated to report it.

While working at the *Constitution*, I didn't have to look far. Corruption in Georgia was so ingrained and so brazen, it offered an embarrassment of riches for someone of my bent. Over the next dozen years, I wrote about speed traps in Ludowici, gambling parlors in Savannah, police-protected whorehouses in Athens, criminally negligent conditions at Milledgeville State Hospital, election fraud in Telfair County, truck stop brothels in Rome, marriage mills on the Georgia-Florida border, state payroll padding, embezzlement of tax funds, use of convict labor for private work, and on and on.

Sometimes the corruption was positively laughable, like the purchasing scandal I covered in which the state was purchasing boats with no bottoms for lakes with no water. Another time, I turned up a missing road scraper belonging to the state that the Georgia Bureau of Investigation had been trying to find for two years. The *Constitution* helpfully published a map showing the GBI where the scraper was located. The next day, a sheepish GBI retrieved it and fined the contractor who'd been using it several thousand dollars for "borrowing" state property.

The *Constitution* played the hell out of my stories and they ran full-page house ads with my photo, listing the prizes I had won. I don't think I realized it then, but it now seems clear that the editors were using my prominence to promote the paper—an early exercise in what's now known as branding. It was also a way of snatching bragging rights from the *Journal*, which had its own crackerjack investigative reporter, namely John Pennington. (It was Pennington who set Carter on the road to the presidency by uncovering the massive vote fraud that led to him losing a primary election for state senator in 1962. Carter sued and was ultimately declared the victor and went on to win the general election.)

All of the publicity was turning me into something of a personality in the state—a rarity for a newspaper reporter in those days before TV began minting celebrity journalists by the dozen. I enjoyed the attention, but there was a bigger payoff. The more well known I became, the more it made people eager to cooperate with me. Some of my best stories started with phone calls from people who'd read my exposés and were upset about corruption of one kind or another. They knew there was not much point in going to the authorities, because so many officials were corrupt themselves. That was why Brigadier General Mayo, whose complaints about the vice surrounding Camp Stewart were ignored by the authorities, turned to me. I got so many credible leads that I usually kept three investigations going at any one time and still had a long backlog of cases to investigate.

It was also extremely gratifying to see how many of my articles—dozens of them over the years—resulted in major reforms and/or investigations by state and federal grand juries. Knowing that my work was having so much impact as well as attracting wide readership drove me to work long hours, usually to the exclusion of anything else except for my college courses at night. Often, I put in more than eighty hours a week and would be gone on weekends. I needed the overtime pay, because by 1955 Virginia and I had filled out our family with three children who arrived in quick succession. There was Karen, who, as I mentioned, was born in 1952. Next came Mike, born sixteen months later, in November 1953. Then Steve came just fourteen months after Mike. They were beautiful, healthy, lively children, but they didn't see a lot of me. I remember the time when Karen was about six or seven, she and the two boys put up a sign on the lawn that said "Welcome Home Daddy." But my absences became so routine the kids stopped paying much attention to my comings and goings.

Virginia bore the brunt of it. It was years before she and I took any vacation, and even that wasn't a real vacation. We went to Jekyll Island for a week so that I could work on a series of stories. At home, the phone was always ringing; uninterrupted meals were practically unheard of. After dinner, I would spend hours on the phone, checking details of stories or taking calls from tipsters. Sometimes a tip would send me out again at night, regardless of the hour. And there were endless crank calls, which were generally more of a nuisance but occasionally were frightening.

Transportation was another major problem for her. I often had to use the family car for days at a time on out-of-town assignments, making it difficult to get the kids back and forth to school. The situation improved somewhat after she joined a car pool, but many a time she had to depend on somebody else to fill in for her because I was using the car.

While I look back on all that with regret, what pains me the most is the fact that I missed out on so much of the growing up of my children. I loved them dearly, and I don't think they ever doubted that, but it was the rare occasion when I had time to help with homework or play catch with the boys in the backyard. I was too busy chasing crooked sheriffs and state officials with their hands in the till.

There was of course, a bigger story at the time, but it didn't occur to me that I could be using my investigative techniques to expose the harsh system of white supremacy in the Deep South. All of this, as I mentioned, was fine with my editors at the *Constitution*, who were determined to ignore "the situation" as much as they could.

There were some racial stories the *Constitution* couldn't ignore. In 1957, I was in Montgomery, Alabama, doing a follow-up on the Montgomery bus boycott which had ended the previous year, when I got an urgent call from Managing Editor Fields telling me to leave immediately for Little Rock, Arkansas. President Eisenhower had just ordered federal troops into Little Rock to protect black students enrolled in Central High School under a federal court desegregation order. (Playing me up as always, the *Constitution* ran a front-page article headlined "Jack Nelson Covering the Little Rock Story.")

With Governor Orville Faubus leading resistance to desegregation, violence had broken out, and more was expected when the school was scheduled to open the next morning. It was an all-night drive from Montgomery to Little Rock under the best of circumstances and I exceeded the speed limit much of the time. Outside a small town in north Mississippi, about 150 miles from Little Rock, a beefy officer wearing a police chief's badge pulled me over.

"You come into this town goin' mighty fast, boy, and you left it goin' mighty fast," he said. "Just where you goin', boy?"

"Chief," I said, pulling out my driver's license and handing it to him, "I'm a reporter for the *Atlanta Constitution*. I'm headed for Little Rock to cover the desegregation of the high school. President Eisenhower has ordered troops in and I'm trying to get there before they do."

He looked at my driver's license and broke into a wide grin. "Tell you what you do, boy," he said, handing the license back to me. "You kill me a nigger up there and I'll let you go."

"Okay, chief," I said, thanking him for not charging me. As I drove carefully away, I thought how lucky I'd been. Obviously the chief had never heard of Ralph McGill or the *Constitution*'s reputation as a liberal paper.

I reached Little Rock at dawn on September 25, 1957, just as trucks of the 102nd Airborne Division were rumbling into the city. And I covered the desegregation crisis there. But like most other reporters for southern newspapers, I covered it mostly as a police action story, the way Fields wanted me to, reporting on the number of civilians injured and arrested and how the troops were deployed, etc. I failed to delve into the white power structure's role and its racist policies, and I ignored the underlying situation which had made it necessary for President Eisenhower to send in federal troops with fixed bayonets to confront potentially violent segregationists.

In contrast to reporters from some segregationist papers whose reporting reflected their papers' strong opposition to the civil rights movement, I at least played it straight in writing about the confrontation between state and federal powers in Little Rock. The *Nashville Banner's* staff-written anti-integration stories were datelined: "With the Federal Occupation Forces in Little Rock." A columnist for the Jackson, Mississippi, *Clarion-Ledger* suggested that flame-throwers be used to deter civil rights demonstrators at the scene. And southern television stations had their own biases: two NBC affiliates in the South dropped the Huntley-Brinkley news report because of John Chancellor's aggressive but accurate reporting out of Little Rock.

I recall sympathizing with the ordeal the black kids integrating the high school had to face, and I was appalled by Faubus's race-baiting. But Little Rock was fundamentally a diversion for me from what I saw as my real work: uncovering the massive corruption back in Georgia.

Chapter 10

A SNAKE PIT CALLED MILLEDGEVILLE

IN TWELVE YEARS of intensive investigative reporting that involved hundreds of stories, I made a lot of enemies. I was physically attacked twice—once by the deputy sheriff in Hinesville, once by a doctor—and threatened many times. Among other things, I was denounced as a skunk, a little bastard, a lying son of a bitch, a hatchet man—described as "a cross between a sadist and a rattlesnake"—and a joree, a bird that digs up worms from under rocks.

It was Marvin Griffin, governor of Georgia from 1955 to 1959, who came up with the term joree for me. He also referred to me as a ubiquitous scribbler. The fact is, he gave me a lot to write about. An archsegregationist and an egregious crook, he believed in rewarding his friends and punishing his enemies. His cronies were awarded lucrative state business—purchasing contracts, highway construction projects, and the like. His enemies got something else.

I remember state representative George Bagby declaring on the house floor that he had heard that if he didn't vote for one of Griffin's programs, the governor would fire his brother from the highway department. But Bagby said that was all right, his brother could come on home and wouldn't starve without a state job because "we got ham in the smokehouse and meal in the barrel to make a hoecake." Griffin got word of Bagby's speech and sent him this message: "Dear George, Get the ham out of the smokehouse and the meal out of the barrel and make a hoecake. Your brother's coming home."

If Griffin got furious with me and the paper, it was no wonder. During his administration, we churned out almost daily news accounts of wrongdoing in most of the large departments of state government—highways, revenue, purchasing, parks, corrections, health, and welfare. Other exposés focused on the cronyism and nepotism in his administration:

Marvin's brother, Cheney, routinely accepted bribes from businessmen seeking access to the governor. It helped to bring along a box of cigars, too. With more than thirty indictments of officials in his administration returned, *Reader's Digest* ran a story saying that "[n]ever had so many stolen so much in so short a time."

Griffin and his allies made several attempts at retaliation against the Atlanta papers, succeeding in curtailing liquor advertising and passing a law making it easier to sue the larger papers in the state—moves that were eventually overturned. For all that, Griffin was a good-humored crook who couldn't stay mad. Years after leaving office, he was having a few drinks with me and some other journalists, and he started reminiscing.

"Jack, do you know what I used to think to myself every time I had a press conference in the governor's office and I'd see you coming through the door with that damned notebook in your hand?" he asked.

"No, governor," I said. "What was that?"

"I'd think, 'I wonder what that beady-eyed son of a bitch has got on me this week.'"

Given the nature of my stories, it's not surprising that the *Constitution* and I were threatened repeatedly with libel suits. But despite the threats, no libel suit was ever filed, a result, I think, of efforts to scrupulously stick to the facts and document all allegations.

Thinking back on the many pressures the paper faced, constantly fending off lawsuits, boycotts, and angry readers, I'd say the *Constitution* of that era acquitted itself very well. The paper certainly stood behind me, and so did Bill Fields, who never tried to rein me in. Sour and tight-lipped as he was, he did not inspire much love in the newsroom. But he had sound journalistic instincts, and on those occasions when he raised questions, they were legitimate ones. The *Constitution* also had a libel lawyer, Barmore Gambrell, who, unlike lawyers for many newspapers, looked for ways to approve publication of stories rather than nitpicking them for possible libel and rejecting them. I give him a lot of credit for keeping us out of trouble by the thorough way he vetted every ticklish fact. He believed—and I agreed with him—there should be no margin for error in investigative stories alleging criminal or unethical conduct.

I was scrupulous about documenting everything and learned early to zero in on records. Patience has never been one of my virtues, and there's nothing more tedious than poring through files hour after hour. But when you get your hands on the right record, you have a piece of evidence that can't be denied.

I discovered another way to ward off lawsuits: sworn affidavits—a tool strongly endorsed by Gambrell. Once a source agreed to sign an affidavit, I would draft a document that followed a simple formula. In it, the source would declare he was making the sworn statement of his own free will without any kind of coercion or reward or promise of reward, followed by a statement of the allegations and ending with a declaration that the source had read the statement carefully and was willing to swear to its contents. The affidavits were quite detailed. I got them typed up when I could. At other times, I might be forced to handwrite something in a barnyard. The next step was to find a notary public to administer the oath and notarize the signatures. Usually this was not a problem because notaries could be found in banks, law offices, insurance companies, and other businesses.

To my knowledge, newspapers have seldom used affidavits, either in those days or in more recent times. I found them so useful, I don't really understand why it hasn't been a more common practice.

It's not as if people fell all over themselves to give me affidavits; it was especially difficult in the beginning. I had to convince sources they could have confidence in what I was doing and that a sworn statement was necessary to show that the newspaper would publish serious allegations only when they were backed by substantial evidence. I focused so heavily on getting affidavits and drew up so many in my years at the *Constitution* that the paper's regular readers became accustomed to seeing stories based on them. On some occasions I had people offer to give me affidavits before I even asked, and some sources volunteered to get others to sign affidavits to support their allegations.

I used the names of people who signed affidavits if they were willing for me to let them be named. But I struck agreements with other sources to keep their names confidential unless allegations contained in the affidavits resulted in a libel suit and their testimony was needed to defend the *Constitution* in court.

While I can't recall exactly why I began drafting affidavits, I remember that a source in a local corruption case suggested he would be willing to swear to what he was telling me, so I drew up an affidavit for him to sign. What I do clearly recall is that I became sold on affidavits after the first one because they strengthened my stories and protected the newspaper from libel suits or complaints by sources that they had been misquoted.

I was thankful I had collected affidavits in what was probably the most memorable investigation of my career: the horrific conditions at

Milledgeville State Hospital. In 1959, Milledgeville was the world's largest mental institution, with an astounding 15,000 patients—12,500 in the hospital and 2,500 out-patients. It all started with a phone call to Managing Editor Fields from Philip Chandler, a state legislator from Milledgeville.

Chandler asked Fields to look into reports of terrible conditions and widespread corruption at the hospital and asked if he would assign the reporter "who dug up the story about the road scandal down at Baxley." I had written a series of stories about corruption involving state highway department funds, including some used to pave streets and sidewalks in Baxley that were never paved. To give the story more wattage, the contractor was the mayor and a close friend of the governor.

Over the years the state mental hospital had been widely known as "a snake pit," and the press and the Georgia legislature had investigated it several times. But their reports, mostly confined to overcrowding, underfunding, and poor treatment, never resulted in serious reform. As the only state mental hospital in Georgia, it had steadily grown over the years into a sprawling, miserable warehouse for humans. And politicians, as well as the medical profession, generally found it easier to ignore its myriad problems or pay lip service to reform rather than provide the funding and expertise to deal effectively with them.

My investigation, aided by Chandler and several doctors and other employees on the hospital staff, documented not only appalling conditions but specific examples of malpractice and other hair-raising corruption that either endangered the lives of many patients or killed them outright. I wrote a series of stories showing that while the hospital had a huge backlog of surgical cases, a female nurse was actually performing major surgery on patients, including hip operations that even some surgeons were not considered qualified to perform. Meanwhile, the chief surgeon, Dr. Wallace Gibson, who had a close relationship with the nurse, often spent his time performing operations on patients at a private, for-profit hospital operated by a friend, sometimes taking with him surgical instruments that were needed for operations at the state hospital.

Another staff doctor, Zeb Burrell, who also was working as a paid consultant for a pharmaceutical firm, had been using experimental drugs on mental patients without their knowledge or the knowledge of their relatives or guardians. The doctor made no accounting to the hospital for payments to him or for the research program financed by the drug firm.

From checking records and sources I found that for the hospital's fifteen thousand patients there were only forty-eight doctors—not one a psychiatrist—and twelve had histories of alcoholism or drug addiction backgrounds. The hospital superintendent, Dr. T. G. Peacock, had actually hired several of them off the mental wards. And he had kept on the staff several doctors who had been discovered to be under the influence of narcotics or alcohol while on duty. In several cases doctors on the institution's staff were confined at the hospital for treatment of mental illness before being returned to duty.

Finally, a purchasing scandal involving kickbacks to hospital and state officials created a situation in which the hospital's average expenditure per patient for housing, food, and health care was a paltry $2.52 a day.

With the help of sources on the inside, I was able to convincingly document most of the abuses, but I didn't get everything handed to me on a silver platter. The allegation that a nurse was performing major surgery was a bombshell, but I had only one affidavit to support it. It came from an operating room technician, Buford Quinn, who at that time chose to remain anonymous for job security reasons. He swore he had seen the nurse performing hip-nail operations. But Barmore Gambrell said that in order for him to sign off on publishing the story we needed at least one more witness to sign an affidavit swearing he could attest to the operations. I tried to find another witness who was willing to sign an affidavit but finally told Gambrell I couldn't come up with one.

Gambrell asked if I could find a staff doctor who knew Buford Quinn and would sign an affidavit swearing he would believe any sworn statement Quinn made. I discussed it with Dr. Thomas Phinizy, one of several doctors who had given me affidavits alleging wrongdoing at the hospital, and he signed another affidavit saying he would believe anything Quinn said under oath. On the basis of that affidavit we published the charge that a nurse had performed major surgery.

At first Dr. Peacock had declined my requests for an interview, but after the first couple of articles were published, I went to the superintendent's office and was admitted for what turned out to be an extraordinary and rather chilling interview. Peacock was furious and flew into a rage, cursing me, Ralph McGill, and the *Constitution*. "We don't mind decent people and papers," he said, "but when they come on fishing expeditions, they stink—and so does your paper and your editor-in-chief." At one point, he interrupted the interview to take a telephone call from Dr. Gibson, the chief surgeon.

"Yeah," Peacock told Gibson. "I've got that fella Jack Nelson from that lyin' Ralph McGill, communist-lovin', nigger-lovin' *Atlanta Constitution* in my office right now. He ought to be turned over to those patients that handled that other fellow." Of course, every word he said to me appeared in the *Constitution* the next morning.

How those patients took care of that "other fellow" or who that fellow was I never learned. But Dr. Charles Jordan, who operated a private hospital nearby where Dr. Gibson sometimes performed surgery, tried to "handle" me some time later when I showed up at a meeting of the Baldwin County Medical Society in Milledgeville where my articles were being discussed. When I attempted to cover the meeting, Dr. Jordan, his face twisted in rage, bellowed, "You are persecuting one of the finest men in the county," then slugged me several times before other doctors pulled him away. The next day, the *Constitution* ran a front-page story with my photo headlined, "Jack Nelson Is Slugged by Doctor."

To say that many of the state's doctors were upset by my reporting would be putting it mildly. The Baldwin County Medical Society passed a resolution condemning me and the *Constitution*, charging us with unfairly criticizing doctors and the hospital. The Fulton County (Atlanta) Medical Society followed up by unanimously passing a resolution protesting the stories and sent a delegation of doctors to the *Constitution* to lecture the editors on assigning a nonmedical person to draw conclusions and write stories about a medical institution.

Dr. Jordan's attack gave me a swollen jaw, but the attack was a blessing in disguise because the story prompted more people to call me with information about irregularities at the hospital. Hospital sources gave me affidavits showing that, despite a surgical backlog of several hundred patients, many persons ineligible for surgery at the hospital, including some from out of state, had undergone operations there. Unqualified persons administered X-rays, and, in many cases, unqualified people administered anesthesia to patients. Negro patients were treated even more harshly than whites, and after surgery they were shuttled off to a clinic about a mile away because they were not permitted to stay in the building housing the operating rooms.

Not all of the ensuing reaction to my stories was negative. After the initial series and the interview with Peacock were published, the *Journal of the Medical Association of Georgia* reported that "[c]itizens throughout the state were shocked" and editorialized in favor of sweeping reforms. An embarrassed Ernest Vandiver, Marvin Griffin's successor as governor, asked the medical association to appoint a committee to investigate the allegations. The resulting committee of doctors held closed-door hearings at the hospital and interviewed some of the same witnesses I had quoted.

At one of the hearings I was standing close enough to a door leading to the hearing room to hear testimony by Alan Kemper, the crusty old director of the state welfare department, which administered the hospital. At one point he bellowed that "that Jack Nelson from the *Constitution* can cut my guts out but he'll pay for every drop of blood. He's a hatchet man, and that's a cross between a sadist and a rattlesnake."

The public's spontaneous reaction to the Milledgeville series that engulfed Georgia was unexpected and stirred action from many quarters. Governor Vandiver and his wife toured the hospital. She wept at what she saw. Legislators and their wives also went through the back wards, which some officials who were veterans of World War II likened to conditions at Nazi concentration camps. Hundreds of letters were written to the editors of Georgia newspapers, while state officials, lawmakers, mental health leaders, and civic organizations demanded action.

Seeing the groundswell mount, the *Constitution* embarked on an all-out crusade—the old-fashioned kind you rarely see any more except on the part of right-wing radio talk hosts and Fox television personalities. Fields assigned several other reporters to develop mental health stories, while I was dispatched to Topeka, Kansas, to do a series on the famed Menninger Clinic. The purpose was to show how in ten years Kansas jumped from near the bottom to the top in psychiatric care. For months, the paper ran daily news stories, editorials, and editorial cartoons on Milledgeville and the field of mental health generally. I got personally involved too, giving dozens of speeches to community and medical groups, arguing passionately for better care for the mentally ill.

Finally, after a lengthy investigation, the doctors' committee issued a scathing report that confirmed all the allegations and concluded that Kemper and Peacock had followed a conscious policy of recruiting doctors with alcohol or drug addiction backgrounds and had hired some who had been only "partially rehabilitated." The report called for widespread reform including moving the hospital from Kemper's welfare department to the health department. The fallout from the report also swept Dr. Peacock, Dr. Gibson, and several other doctors out of the hospital.

All of the pressure from so many quarters eventually brought more humane treatment and better health care for the patients. Many reforms were instituted, including a $12 million program to downsize Milledgeville and build regional mental health facilities around the state. I can't think of another story I covered that had such far-reaching consequences.

Chapter 11

DEAD MEN VOTING

THE MILLEDGEVILLE SERIES was a turning point in my career. Not only could I take pride in the bettering of treatment for thousands of mental patients; I also won the Pulitzer Prize for local reporting under deadline pressure. While I was proud of the award, I learned later how lucky I was to win it. The Medical Association of Georgia had nominated me for the prize in the reporting category, but Bill Fields got the Georgia Press Association to nominate the newspaper for a Pulitzer for public service.

Many years later, while going through the Pulitzer Prize archives at Columbia University in connection with a story I was writing, I came upon a letter from Fields to the Pulitzer Advisory Committee saying that at the committee's request he was forwarding several doctors' letters supporting me for the Pulitzer. But he emphasized that he still thought the award should go to the *Constitution* rather than me.

Benjamin McKelway, a member of the committee, later told me that in the initial voting for the Gold Medal for Public Service, the *Constitution* was tied, five to five, with the *Los Angeles Times*, the newspaper I would join five years later. The *Times* had published a powerful series on drug smuggling from Mexico. To break the deadlock between the *Constitution* and the *Times*, McKelway had suggested the committee give the Gold Medal for Public Service to the *Times* and award the Pulitzer for local reporting to me because I had done all the reporting on the Milledgeville series. And that is what happened. McKelway said the fact that I had been a finalist for the Pulitzer the two preceding years—for the series on a police-protected Atlanta lottery ring and stories on corruption in the Griffin administration—also figured in the advisory committee's decision. Getting the Pulitzer was heady stuff. Besides the personal satisfaction of helping to right wrongs, I was being recognized nationally for my work. (A few people were not bowled over. When MawMaw, my grandmother, heard I'd received the Pulitzer, she said, "That's nice. Maybe next time he'll win the Nobel.") I was even a guest on *I've Got a Secret*, then a very popular show. During rehearsals, I was surprised to learn that the show was completely rehearsed, and the panelists knew the identity of the guests before they went on the air. After I got back home, I wrote a lighthearted exposé, but I'll bet Garry Moore and the producers were not amused.

The Pulitzer would have a dramatic impact on my life, but that would come a bit later. For the time being, I was deeply immersed in my investigations. And truth to tell, I was enjoying the hell out of my role as a kind of journalistic avenger, striking fear into the heart of crooked officials. I even got another nickname. When locals in various places heard I was sniffing around, they used to say, "Uh-oh. The booger man is back in town."

Not long after wrapping up my Milledgeville coverage, I zeroed in on Telfair County in south Georgia. Home of the politically powerful Talmadges—Gene and his son Herman—the county was notorious over the years for vote fraud. George Goodwin, an *Atlanta Journal* reporter, won a Pulitzer Prize in 1948 for exposing widespread fraud that included casting ballots in the names of people long dead whose names had remained on the rolls of registered voters. Thereafter, opponents of the Talmadges' political machine continued to complain of vote fraud.

In 1960, with former governor Herman Talmadge by then serving in the U.S. Senate, I was tipped off that once again officials were planning to stuff the ballot boxes to keep the courthouse gang in power. The tipster was a man named Pete Yawn, a political opponent of the gang. At my request, Yawn arranged for me to meet with a group of his friends before the election, and they agreed that they would, as discreetly as possible, keep an accurate count of the number of persons who voted in Milan, a key precinct.

Yawn stood outside the polling place in Milan on election day with a counting device in his pocket, clicking it every time a voter came out of the building. At various times during the day, Yawn noted his own count and asked political friends who showed up to vote to give him the numbers of their ballot stubs. His tally at 9 a.m. showed only 47 people had voted, but the 47th person had a ballot stub numbered 118. By the time the polls closed, his count was 295. The final tabulation for the precinct was 664, or 369 more than Yawn had counted. But we didn't go with the story right away. We needed names of the phantom voters.

After the election, we obtained a list of names from the secretary of state's office of people who were supposed to have voted in the precinct. With Yawn and his friends, who knew personally almost everyone living in the precinct, we went over every name on the list. They pointed out the names of people who were dead—tombstone voting, we called it in Georgia in those days—as well as scores of others who were nonexistent or who had long since moved away from the county. The list also contained the names of many eligible voters who had not actually voted that day.

Armed with these leads, I drove around the county, interviewing scores of witnesses and collecting affidavits, some from farmers that I wrote out in longhand which I still have. One was from the widow of a man who had been dead for ten years. She swore she hadn't voted either—that she was sick that day, although her name appeared on the list of voters. The result was a series of five page-one articles outlining charges of widespread vote fraud—multiple voting of one name, voting of fictitious names, tombstone voting, and so on. There were massive irregularities in other precincts too. In one, the number of votes officially tabulated was 664 even though I had an affidavit from a man who tabulated votes in that precinct and swore only 295 persons had cast ballots.

The articles touched off FBI and federal grand jury investigations, infuriating Talmadge cronies who were Telfair officials. One of them—Jack Walker, chairman of the Telfair Democratic Executive Committee—hurried to Washington where Senator Talmadge arranged for him to meet with Attorney General Robert Kennedy. Walker told Kennedy any investigation should be left to the county grand jury. As I pointed out in an article, it just so happened that Walker was a member of the Telfair grand jury and was a nephew of Charles Walker, one of the election officials in the precinct where much of the vote fraud occurred.

Kennedy was noncommittal about the status of the federal investigation so Jack Walker returned to Telfair County where the local grand jury subpoenaed witnesses I had quoted and the affidavits they had given me. The jury then issued a presentment saying that while it found irregularities, there were no grounds for indictments. However, Kennedy had pressed ahead with the Justice Department's investigation and the federal grand jury ultimately returned a sealed indictment.

Since the indictment was sealed, I didn't have much of a story. I was drowning my sorrows at a bar in nearby Savannah Beach when I was paged for a telephone call. On the phone was Edwin O. Guthman, Kennedy's public information aide, whom I had never met, but who had tracked me down in the bar because he knew I had written the stories that prompted the federal investigation. In fact, in an earlier telephone interview, he had disclosed the fact that Talmadge's office was trying to get Kenendy to call off the federal investigation.

"Jack, I know you wrote the stories that caused the Telfair fraud investigation," he said, "and I know that the sealed indictment doesn't give you much of a story. While I can't tell you the names of those who were indicted, I can tell you on background that fifteen election officials were indicted. You can quote me as an authoritative source, but not by name." I thanked him profusely, rushed to a telephone, and dictated a story with a Savannah dateline that ran under a page-one, three-column headline and began like this:

"A federal grand jury here returned a sealed indictment Monday charging conspiracy in the Telfair County vote fraud investigation. The *Constitution* learned from an authoritative source late Monday night that about 15 persons are named in the indictment."

It was five years later, after I had opened the Atlanta bureau of the *Los Angeles Times,* that I next heard from Ed Guthman. He had just been named national editor of the *Times,* which meant I would be reporting to him. He had been a great public servant and was a courageous journalist who had won a Pulitzer Prize at the *Seattle Times* for clearing a college professor of charges he had attended a Communist training school. He was as tough as they come and took a great interest in my work. I was proud to have another distinguished mentor to add to my list.

Jack as a toddler, sitting in front of his grandparents' house in Talladega, Alabama.

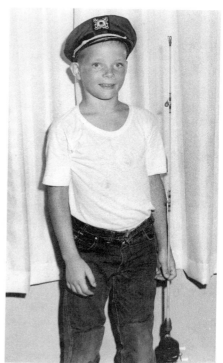

Jack at age eleven. To help make ends meet, he had started going door-to-door, selling iodine, shoestrings, and magazines by the time he was six.

Scrawny Jack was a Golden Gloves champion who was undefeated in high school.

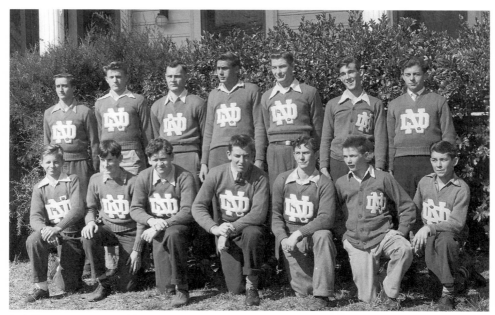

Jack (bottom row, second from right) was sports-crazy in high school. He deliberately tried to flunk his senior year in order to come back and play quarterback again.

Jack with his sister, Barbara, brother, Kenny, and Barbara, his mother. She was a widow by that time; Jack's father had been struck and killed by an automobile when Jack was sixteen.

Horsing around with his buddies from Biloxi's Battery C at Camp Stewart, now Fort Stewart, Georgia.

Jack as a sergeant in the National Guard at Camp Stewart, Georgia. He managed to stay out of Korea by writing glowing press releases about the commanding officer.

Twenty-one-year-old Jack, interviewing Biloxi Mayor G. B. Cousins in his office in 1950. Jack's editor at the *Daily Herald* told him he'd go far because he wasn't afraid to make people mad.

Jack moonlighted at the *Savannah Morning News* and other Georgia papers while at Camp Stewart. The editor of the *Atlanta Constitution* liked his work so much he offered him a job when his tour of duty was up.

When Jack was ready to be discharged from the National Guard, his superiors discovered that, thanks to his work as a public information supervisor, he had never done any basic training.

Jack married Virginia Dare Dickinson in a military ceremony in the base chapel. Her parents, who did not approve of his Catholicism, did not attend.

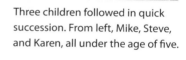

Three children followed in quick succession. From left, Mike, Steve, and Karen, all under the age of five.

In the *Atlanta Constitution* newsroom in 1958.

Mike and Steve try out their dad's typewriter in the newsroom of the *Atlanta Constitution*.

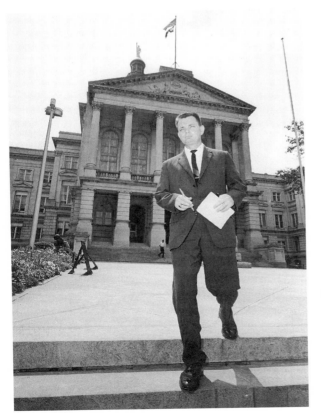

In the 1950s, Jack, seen here in front of the state capitol, broke stories almost daily about corruption in the administration of Governor Marvin Griffin. *Reader's Digest* ran a story at the time saying, "Never had so many stolen so much in so short a time."

Jack's revelations about conditions at the Milledgeville mental hospital prompted a flood of awards, including this one being presented by Georgia Governor Ernest Vandiver.

THE TRUSTEES OF COLUMBIA UNIVERSITY
IN THE CITY OF NEW YORK
TO ALL PERSONS TO WHOM THESE PRESENTS MAY COME GREETING
BE IT KNOWN THAT

JACK NELSON

has been awarded

THE PULITZER PRIZE IN JOURNALISM
FOR DISTINGUISHED LOCAL REPORTING
UNDER DEADLINE PRESSURE

IN ACCORDANCE WITH THE PROVISIONS OF THE STATUTES OF THE UNIVERSITY GOVERNING SUCH AWARD

IN WITNESS WHEREOF WE HAVE CAUSED THIS CERTIFICATE TO BE SIGNED BY THE PRESIDENT OF THE UNIVERSITY AND OUR CORPORATE SEAL TO BE HERETO AFFIXED IN THE CITY OF NEW YORK ON THE SECOND DAY OF MAY IN THE YEAR OF OUR LORD ONE THOUSAND NINE HUNDRED AND SIXTY

PRESIDENT

The Pulitzer Prize Jack won in 1960 for exposing the abuses at Milledgeville State Hospital. The series resulted in widespread reforms in the care of Georgia's mental patients.

With Bess Myerson and Betsy Palmer on *I've Got a Secret* in 1960. His secret was that he'd won the Pulitzer Prize.

Jack with two giants of southern journalism, Eugene Patterson, left, and Ralph McGill in the center. Jack and McGill had already won Pulitzer Prizes. They are congratulating Patterson on winning one for commentary.

Jack, at far left, plunged into coverage of civil rights with the same zeal with which he had chased down crooked sheriffs in Georgia.

Having written a story calling Bogalusa, Louisiana, "the meanest town in the South," Jack was warned by police not to return. He took their advice.

After moving to Washington in 1969, Jack took on J. Edgar Hoover and his FBI. Hoover retaliated forcefully, trying to get Jack fired.

Jack and Barbara at their wedding in Philadelphia in 1974.

Interviewing Fidel Castro in Havana in the late seventies. Jack was outspoken in his view that the United States ought to recognize Cuba.

Jack invented "the bureau breakfast," bringing in high-level government officials to meet with bureau reporters. The guest on this particular day was Jimmy Carter's attorney general, Griffin Bell. Jack is flanked by two of the bureau's top investigative reporters, Robert Jackson (on left) and Ronald Ostrow.

In an interview with Jack in the Oval Office, Ronald Reagan blithely ignored his press secretary, Larry Speakes (in rear), who kept trying, without success, to bring the session to an end.

Reporting on Ronald Reagan's trip to China in 1984.

Jack with son Steve, who died in 1996, grandson Casey, and Barbara, his mother, known to all as Mama Bob.

Terror in the Night, Jack's true-life thriller about the Klan's campaign against the Jews of Mississippi, has been optioned several times by various Hollywood writers and directors.

Jack buttonholes California Congressman Jerome Waldie, a member of the House Judiciary Committee, during the Watergate impeachment hearings. The trio of Jack Nelson, Ron Ostrow, and Bob Jackson helped keep the *Los Angeles Times* competitive with Bob Woodward and Carl Bernstein, the *Washington Post*'s ace reporters.

Jack with Paul Duke (center), moderator of *Washington Week in Review*, and Charlie McDowell of the *Richmond Times-Dispatch*. The three were good friends both on and off the air.

Jack gained prominence from his frequent appearances on television, particularly PBS's *Washington Week in Review*. From left: Jack, Harry Ellis of the *Christian Science Monitor*, *Washington Week* moderator Paul Duke, syndicated columnist Georgie Anne Geyer, and Charlie McDowell of the *Richmond Times-Dispatch*.

Jack with President Jimmy Carter at a panel discussion hosted by *National Geographic* in 2000. Jack had an inside track when Carter, a fellow Georgian, was in the White House. They knew each other from the time Carter served as a state senator.

At the end of his interview with Vice President George H. W. Bush, Jack complained that he hadn't told him a single newsworthy thing. The vice president replied, "Yeah, but look where it's gotten me."

Jack could get some presidents on the phone easier than others. Bill Clinton was unusually accessible.

Jack surrounded by five of his six grandchildren. From left, Casey, Robin, Kelly, and Krystal. Jack is holding the youngest, Lindsay. Kayla had not yet been born.

Jack and Barbara on a trip to Alaska in 2004.

A tremendous booster of the *Los Angeles Times*, Jack bridled when people said the *Times*, meaning the *New York Times*. He was quick to remind them that there was another *Times*, the one based in Los Angeles.

Jack as portrayed by Paul Conrad, the *Los Angeles Times'* legendary cartoonist. Used by permission of the Conrad estate.

Chapter 12

SIN IN THE CLASSIC CITY

MAYOR RALPH SNOW of Athens sounded highly agitated when he telephoned me one day and asked if I would come over and look into how prostitution, illegal gambling, and liquor sales were victimizing some of the sixty-three hundred students at the University of Georgia. Athens billed itself as the Classic City and was especially proud of the university, the nation's oldest state-chartered university, founded in 1875.

The mayor was particularly upset about four houses of prostitution he said were catering to students, including many minors. He told me he had been offered a four-hundred-dollar-a-week bribe to allow the houses to continue to operate. "I rejected the bribe and informed the man who offered it—a prominent Athens businessman—that I would do everything in my power to keep the houses from operating," he said.

And then he added, "We've also got a slot machine factory over here and slot machines at private clubs and other places that are taking a lot of money from our students. I can't trust my own police department. Can you come over here and write about what's going on?"

That commercial vice was flourishing in Athens in 1960 was not exactly a secret. In fact, the Athens political establishment had winked at illegal gambling and prostitution for years, and some of the city's most prominent citizens, including university officials and faculty members, were members of private clubs where minors drank liquor and played slot machines. But what worried Snow—and what much of the public apparently didn't realize—was that Athens had become the slot machine center of Georgia and that gambling, prostitution, and liquor sales increasingly were aimed at students. Nor did the public know that Snow had been offered a bribe to let the houses of prostitution operate and that an Athens businessman operated an illegal slot machine factory and distributed the devices to private clubs in many other counties across the state.

Snow felt that if the *Constitution* exposed these facts the public would support his efforts to clean up the situation. I told him I would do what I could, not realizing at the time that I would wind up having to talk myself out of what you could say was a potentially compromising position in a whorehouse.

Bill Young, a *Constitution* photographer, was assigned to accompany me on visits to private clubs where university students were playing slot machines. Using a concealed camera he photographed students gambling and I interviewed several who had suffered substantial losses. He also photographed a policeman in uniform conferring with a mechanic working on one of the slot machines. We followed the mechanic back to the Chambers Music Company and found it was a front for a slot machine factory. I checked federal records in Washington and found that W. A. Chambers, the high-living head of the company, had registered with the Justice Department under a law which required all manufacturers and dealers of gambling devices to register if engaged in interstate transportation.

A confidential source gave me an affidavit swearing that as many as five hundred to six hundred slot machines were stored at one time in the factory and that hundreds of others were stored in Chambers Music Company facilities in several other counties. Since I also had an affidavit from the mayor about the offer of the bribe and interviews with a couple of students who had patronized one of the whorehouses, I telephoned Bill Fields and told him I was ready to write a series of articles and planned to return to Atlanta.

"Have you been in one of the whorehouses?" he asked.

"No, but I've interviewed a couple of students who've been there and I've got an affidavit from Mayor Snow about the bribe he was offered to let them continue operating," I said.

"But if you haven't been in one you can't say for sure there's a whorehouse," Fields said. "You'd better go in one and make sure."

Bill Young and I were less than enthusiastic about taking on that assignment. If we went into one of the houses how could we leave without becoming entangled in a business proposition we might have trouble getting out of? Bill was particularly worried about that and asked how I thought we should handle it. I told him I wasn't sure but figured we'd think of something when we got there.

College students had told me taxi cabs were constantly carrying clients to and from the houses so we went to a cab stand across from the

Athens Police Department and got in the back seat of the lead taxi. I asked the driver to "line us up with some women."

"I can take you down to the River Street cathouses," he said. "There are three of them. It'll cost you ten bucks each."

"Sure," I said, and he drove off. A few minutes later we drove over an old wooden covered bridge on which was painted, in large red letters, "University of Georgia Students Vote Yes for Effie." Effie was Athens's best-known madam. Her girls had serviced university students for many years, and her cathouse was well known not only to students, but to some faculty members.

About fifty yards past the bridge the cabbie pointed out three small one-story houses in a row and said they were whorehouses.

"Which one would you recommend?" I asked.

"Well, I wouldn't let my dog go in that first one," he said, then pointed out the second one and said, "I'd go in that one. Just tell her number seven sent you."

Bill and I were playing the whole thing by ear and still hadn't thought much about what we would do when we got in the house. But we walked up to the front door and I knocked on it. In a few moments a small, grandmotherly-looking woman with gray hair who appeared to be in her sixties or early seventies opened the door and looked us up and down. "Where you fellows from, and what do you want?" she asked.

"We're from Atlanta and we want some women," I said. "Number seven said to tell you he sent us."

"Come on in," she said, ushering us into a living room where two women who appeared to be in their early twenties were curled up on two chairs watching *Sergeant Bilko* on television. One was a brunette and the other was a bleached blonde. They glanced at us, seemingly annoyed at being interrupted, then looked back at the television.

Bill and I started to sit on either side of a tiny, blanket-wrapped dog on a couch facing the two prostitutes when the madam gruffly said, "Don't sit on my Chihuahua!" We made sure we didn't and glanced over at the girls.

Both were dressed in white blouses and short, flowery skirts, and were barefooted. Neither was especially attractive although they had slim figures and big busts. After an awkward silence that seemed to go on forever but probably lasted only a couple of minutes, the brunette turned to us and said, "There's two of y'all and two of us, let's go."

I pointed to the brunette, who was marginally better looking, and said, "I'll take you." She took me by the hand and led me down the hallway into a bedroom. The blonde took Bill by the hand and led him into an adjacent bedroom.

Making it up as I went along, it suddenly occurred to me I needed a plan to get Bill and me out of the house without consummating a sale. As she closed the door and began raising her skirt over her head a plan suddenly dawned on me. "How much?" I asked. "Ten dollars," she said.

"But how much to take you out all night," I said. "My friend and I agreed we want to take y'all out all night."

"We can't do that, it's against the rules," she said. But I insisted that was all we wanted to do. We both raised our voices and argued about it for a couple of minutes until I heard footsteps coming pitty-pat down the hallway, and then a rap on the door.

"What are y'all doing in there," the madam asked in a loud voice, then barged into the room without waiting for an answer. The brunette said, "He's insisting they take us out somewhere all night and I told him it's against the rules."

"You can't do that," the madam said. "You can't take a girl out from any of the houses in Athens. It's not allowed."

I insisted we were only interested in taking them out all night, but she said, "You can't, it's against the rules."

"But number seven said we could," I lied.

Raising her voice, she said, "He gets paid for what he does, but he doesn't run this house, I do. You pay for one time and do it one time, but you have to do it here."

I walked out of the bedroom and into the hall with the madam and the brunette tagging closely behind me while I insisted loudly, "But my friend and I only wanted to take them out all night." Bill Young had heard me and bolted out of the back bedroom, zipping up his pants. "What's the problem," he said, "what's going on?"

"Bill, I told them we agreed we only wanted to take them out all night," I said. Picking up on the cue right away, he said, "That's right, take 'em out all night or nothing doin."

The madam, who we didn't learn until later was the infamous Effie Mathews, known and even beloved by generations of students and faculty members, insisted we should settle for "a straight date" at her house. But we hurriedly left the house and walked back about a mile or so to our car in downtown Athens.

Once back in Atlanta I wrote a series of six articles that the *Constitution* labeled—rather sensationally but factually—"Sin in the Classic City."

The articles provoked praise and criticism of me and the *Constitution*. Even Mayor Snow, although he described the charges as serious and had tipped me off about the corruption and encouraged me to write about it, crumpled under pressure from constituents who complained the series had given Athens a bad image. He said all citizens of Athens "deplore Nelson trying to picture Athens as a Phenix City" (an Alabama town I and other reporters had written about in the late 1950s, exposing it as corruption-ridden).

Nevertheless, Snow called for an investigation and he and others testified before a Clark County grand jury convened to look into the allegations. I was subpoenaed and agreed to testify although not about confidential sources, only about the accuracy of what I had written. One of the jurors, a university professor, asked me if it wasn't better to know the houses of prostitution were operating, so the university would know where to find its students rather than having them seeking sex "God knows where and we wouldn't know where." I replied that was a matter for the university to decide, that I was only testifying to what I had reported, not what I thought was the best way for the students to seek sex.

The grand jury returned eight indictments, including one against Effie, alleging prostitution and illegal gambling and liquor law violations. It also issued a strong statement calling for strict enforcement of gambling and liquor laws and the closing of the houses of prostitution. The houses were closed, slot machines disappeared from Athens, and sales of alcohol to minors dropped dramatically after a police crackdown.

As for me, while some folks—even Mayor Snow in the end—thought I had done a respectable job of exposing the organized vice that was victimizing students, I was ridiculed by some Athens businessmen and many students and their parents for what they called sensationalism and spoiling the image of the Classic City. The *Red and Black*, the university's student newspaper, carried a cartoon mocking the disclosure of the cathouses. It showed two shady-looking women looking perplexed and swinging their purses while standing across from the Athens Police Department and saying, "But the *Constitution* said they'd be here."

Chapter 13

HARVARD MAN

MY MILLEDGEVILLE SERIES continued to attract favorable attention. In 1960, Sigma Delta Chi, the Society of Professional Journalists, selected the *Constitution* for its prestigious public service award. The award ceremony was to be held in Washington, and Bill Fields assigned me to accompany Ralph McGill to Washington for the presentation.

McGill was seated at the head table, but when it came time to accept the award, he motioned to me and said, "You come up and get it, Jack, you did all the work." It was a magnanimous gesture that turned out to have a considerable impact on my career. I went up to the head table to accept the award, and, when I returned to my table, Clark Mollenhoff, a great investigative reporter for *Look* magazine and the *Des Moines Register and Tribune*, jumped up from his seat, grabbed me by the arm and said, "Jack, strike while the iron's hot. Apply for a Nieman. I'm sure you'll get it. I'll write you a letter of recommendation."

I was an admirer of Clark's work and had helped him with some sources in Georgia for a story he had written on the Ku Klux Klan. But I didn't have the slightest idea what he was talking about. "A Nieman," I said, "what the hell is a Nieman?"

He explained that it was a fellowship for promising young journalists that entitled them to an academic year's study at Harvard University. Clark had been a Nieman Fellow and he was sold on the program as a way for reporters to broaden their interests and contacts and advance their careers. You could study anything you chose, and he painted an inviting picture of special dinners and cheese-and-cracker seminars where Neiman Fellows were treated to lectures and discussions with Harvard professors and leading political personalities.

The program was established in 1938 with funds provided by Agnes Wahl Nieman, widow of the founder of the *Milwaukee Journal*. The

bequest, she stipulated, was "to promote and elevate standards of journalism and educate persons deemed especially qualified. . . ." Every year
a committee composed of leading journalists and Harvard professors
selects about a dozen young journalists for the program. In addition to
providing the opportunity for them to attend classes, the Nieman Foundation pays fellows a modest stipend for living expenses. Some of the
nation's leading reporters and editors have studied at Harvard under
Nieman Fellowships.

Despite my not knowing anything about the program, the idea of studying at Harvard, as well as Clark's enthusiasm for the program, appealed to
me, especially since I had never actually finished college. During much of
the previous seven years, while working full time at the *Constitution*, I had
been going to school at night. But my investigative reporting had become
so all-consuming that I had stopped going to classes while still a couple of
quarters shy of a degree in economics. I thought maybe an academic year
at Harvard would compensate to some extent for my lack of a degree.

I applied for the Nieman in 1961, a year in which the selection committee was apparently hoping to elevate the educational level of southern journalists. Of the eleven reporters selected, six of us were from
the South. While all of us became friends, Gene Roberts Jr., then at the
Raleigh News and Observer, and I established an especially close friendship that continues to this day. He, of course, became one of the twentieth
century's greatest editors, serving as executive editor of the *Philadelphia
Inquirer* for twenty years, during which the paper won nineteen Pulitzer
Prizes, and later serving as managing editor of the *New York Times*. Gene
himself, along with another outstanding journalist, former *Atlanta Constitution* editor Hank Klibanoff, won a Pulitzer Prize for history in 2007
for their seminal book on news coverage of civil rights, *Race Beat: The
Press, the Civil Rights Struggle, and the Awakening of a Nation*.

Uprooting the family from our house in suburban Decatur was not
easy. Virginia was not eager to go north, and the kids had been told to
expect the worst from those perfidious Yankees. I remember how hot it
was the summer we arrived, how stifling it was in the little apartment
we found in suburban Belmont. I sometimes had to take the car, so once
again, Virginia found herself stuck for transportation. The kids didn't like
school. They resented being called "southern fried," and teased for saying "yes, ma'am," or "no, sir" to teachers, which they'd been taught to do
down south. For our part, we thought northerners had atrociously bad
manners.

Initially, I felt intimidated by the grandeur of Harvard and the fact that I was associating with so many better-educated people. But I eagerly attended lectures on political science, sociology, and politics, and welcomed getting to know my talented Nieman classmates. Still, I confess that much of what I heard on the subject of race relations grated on me.

Like Virginia and the kids, I couldn't escape the feeling that we southerners were being looked down on, partly on general principles and partly because the only thing most people seemed to know about the South were the scenes of racial violence they'd seen on TV. This ignorance galled me because I found plenty of racial prejudice up north. I recall once going to a barbershop in Belmont, and the barber, hearing that I was from Atlanta, asked, "How's your nigger problem down there?" Before I could tell him I thought the city was handling the situation pretty well, he said, "I'll tell you one goddamned thing. The minute any of them tries to move in around here, we answer the call like it was a fire bell."

My anger and defensiveness spilled over in a talk I gave at a seminar about northern press coverage of the South, later published in *Nieman Reports*, in which I made some highly questionable statements. While insisting that I was not offering a defense or an excuse for racial discrimination in the South, I proceeded to rip into what I saw as exaggerated and sensationalistic coverage that was lacking in context:

> . . . The main interest of the northern press seems to have been the mobs, bus burning, militant statements by irresponsible segregationists, daring statements by freedom riders. Unquestionably this is all news, much of it big news and so treated by southern as well as northern newspapers. But how many northern newspapers have run definitive articles on some of the enormous problems underlying these various outbursts?
>
> . . . The fear of the outnumbered whites in some areas that the Negroes will wrest political control from them must be explained. While this is no excuse for suppressing voter rights, it is a vital part of the problem and should be taken into account. . . . Another real fear is that the high rates of crime and disease among Negroes will drag down the standards of the white community. In Atlanta, Negroes, comprising a third of the population, commit about ten times more murders. Regardless of the reason for these high rates—the oppression of the Negro, the denial of equal opportunities and the lag in educational and cultural development—the fact remains and it does cause fear among many white southerners.

I also said flatly that the Klan was no longer a factor in the South.

> . . . The Klan is dead. I think every southern Nieman Fellow will tell you the same thing. But it lives on in the minds of some northern newspapers and, of course, in the minds of their readers.

It is embarrassing to read all this now, especially in light of the fact that on September 15, 1963, not so many months after I gave that talk, members of the United Klans of America dynamited the Sixteenth Street Baptist Church in Birmingham, killing four little girls and injuring twenty-two others.

By southern standards, I would have been considered a liberal. I believed in treating blacks decently but that things ought to be separate though equal. At Harvard, it was finally dawning on me that if citizens were going to tax-supported schools, they ought to have equal access to them and that subjugation of the black race was manifestly unfair. Slowly but surely I was catching up to *Brown v. Board of Education*.

A couple of professors were instrumental in changing my attitudes. One was Thomas Pettigrew, a social psychologist whose course on race relations I attended. The first topic he presented in class was lynching, and I feared the mirror he was going to hold up to the South would only reflect the negative. I got so angry in class one day that Professor Pettigrew later said he was afraid I was going to hit him after class. But his reasoned, factual approach to the subject made me more aware of the injustice of segregation and racism, and he and I soon became fast friends.

Frank Freidel, the renowned professor of American history whose course I was taking, influenced me too. He had been on the Nieman selection committee that named me, and we also had become friends. One day, out of the blue, he said, "You know, you should write a book about all the censorship that's going on involving school textbooks." He knew from personal experience about the problem, because he had been working with textbook publishers who were trying to fend off interference from the many pressure groups—mostly right-wing organizations that exerted enormous influence on the content and selection of textbooks.

I told him I had never written a book and knew nothing about writing one. But Freidel, who had read my "Sin in the Classic City" series that was part of my application for the Nieman Fellowship, said, "Don't worry, just write like you did about the whorehouses in Athens, Georgia. Everything will come out just fine." He said he would line me up with his editor, Ned Bradford, editor-in-chief of Little, Brown, if I would consider writing a book on the subject.

It was an intriguing idea, but since I still didn't feel comfortable about undertaking such a project, I discussed it with Gene Roberts. He enthusiastically embraced the idea, and we agreed we would both work on the book if we could get a contract. We did some initial research, and then, at Ned Bradford's invitation, had lunch at Locke-Ober's, the famous Boston restaurant where editors and authors frequently lunch. Gene and I both talked excitedly about how we thought it would be a great public service to expose how pressure groups had so much influence in censoring schoolbooks.

Afterwards, at his Boston office, Bradford offered us a contract with a fifteen-hundred-dollar advance, an amount established authors would have dismissed as a pittance but that we considered a bonanza. Just before signing the contract, however, Bradford wanted assurances that we had already done a considerable amount of research on the subject. "How much research material have you actually compiled?" he asked.

I was feeling a little sheepish because we really had not done much research. But Gene, holding his hand about knee-high and looking Bradford in the eye, said, "Oh, we've got a pile of material about that high."

We signed the contract and walked out of Bradford's office. As we got into the elevator, I turned to Gene, who was smiling wryly. "Good God, Gene, what are you talking about saying we've got a pile of material about that high?" I said. "We've probably got no more than a couple of inches of material."

"Don't worry," Gene grinned, "we'll have a big enough pile before it's over."

Gene was one of the greatest characters and one of the most brilliant men I've ever known. After I joined the *Los Angeles Times* we spent countless hours together driving to demonstrations, trials, and murder scenes in the South, even though we were working for rival newspapers. Much of the time, he would be lost in thought, not speaking for miles on end, just smiling that inscrutable little smile of his. Once as we were driving the back roads of Louisiana I pointed out the window and commented, "That's a hell of a Klan hangout over there." Gene said nothing. Then, about ten miles down the road, he said, "Sure is." I started to say, "Sure is what?" but I realized he was commenting about the Klan hangout.

Working together on the censorship book, we discovered a wealth of material about a serious problem which, although it affected every public school in the country, had been given little attention by the news media. Few books had been written on the subject and our research indicated none at least in the previous twenty-five years.

While investigating a textbook publisher's report of widespread censorship of books in Texas, I called upon a news-service bureau at the state capitol in Austin and asked the reporter on duty what the bureau had in its file on J. Evetts Haley, leader of a militant right-wing, book-banning organization called Texans for America. The blasé answer was, "Nothing. You can't take Haley seriously. He's not worth keeping a file on."

Yet Haley and his Texans for America had led successful censorship campaigns against texts and school library books and helped spark a legislative investigation that turned into a witch hunt. Professors, authors, and publishers of texts were smeared as dupes and willing co-conspirators of the Communists.

Like the news-service bureau, most of the Texas press gave Haley relatively little attention. Perhaps they thought a man who publicly advocated "hanging" Supreme Court Chief Justice Earl Warren, punched a professor in an argument over the movie *Operation Abolition*, and smeared Southern Methodist University as being "tainted with left-wingers" should not be taken seriously.

Whatever the reason for the scant attention given to the Haleyites and others who clamored for censorship, the result was that well-organized forces attacking books in Texas operated with relatively little press attention or organized opposition. As a result, they forced major alterations in many textbooks, banned others, and banned many school library books as well.

We found that in many other states the same thing had happened to some degree. In more than a third of the states in the previous five years, legislatures had taken some kind of action to censor school books.

The more we learned, the more I began to see similarities in the attitudes of the pro-censorship forces, whom I found contemptible, and the racists who were oppressing blacks. In fact, I began to see that these people were often one and the same. As my Neiman year wore on, the more exposure I had to enlightened thinking on the subject of race, the more I began to see that the situation in the South was not only untenable, it was wrong.

In the meantime, Gene Roberts and I, encouraged and advised on the project by Freidel and two other highly respected professors, Arthur Schlesinger Sr. and Theodore Morrison, wound up writing *The Censors and the Schools*. Before Little, Brown published the book in 1963, Professor Schlesinger proofread every chapter, even taking time to meticulously insert a synonym here or there where he decided it might help the flow.

The book came out that spring, during an extended labor strike at the *New York Times*, but generally was met with favorable reviews around the country and remained in print for about ten years. Gene and I heard from many sources that the book was used as a resource by school officials and others to help fight censorship of schoolbooks.

After the Nieman year, Gene returned to the *Raleigh News and Observer* and I resumed investigative reporting at the *Atlanta Constitution* with as much fervor as ever. My kids and my wife breathed a collective sigh of relief. They were overjoyed to be back home and once again in the South.

Chapter 14

THE MURDER OF LEMUEL PENN

ONE DAY AFTER RETURNING from Harvard, I was in the Georgia House of Representatives when the speaker suddenly shouted, "Mr. Doorkeeper, get those niggers out of the white section of the gallery!" Several white house aides rushed over and hustled Julian Bond and other prominent blacks out of the gallery. (After passage of the 1965 Voting Rights Act, Bond, a former Student Nonviolent Coordinating Committee official who was to become a good friend of mine, was elected to the Georgia state senate and more recently served as chairman of the National Association for the Advancement of Colored People.) I was repelled by the incident and wrote a story about it, but my reportorial interests still lay elsewhere.

How it was possible for me to turn my back on the story with the racial unrest exploding all over the South perplexes me now. Since the first sit-ins in Greensboro, North Carolina, in February 1960, the tempo of unrest had been accelerating at warp speed. There were demonstrations and sit-ins in dozens of southern cities, freedom rides, mass arrests, mob violence, dogs, fire hoses, murders. At the same time, the progress of school integration remained at a near standstill, despite the Supreme Court's dictum in 1954.

In July 1962, when I returned home from Harvard, I would only have had to travel to the southwestern part of the state to cover the Albany (pronounced All-BINNY) Movement, where a coalition of civil rights organizations was leading marches to secure the right to register to vote and end segregation. The jails were full of demonstrators, and one illustrious prisoner, Martin Luther King Jr., who was in and out of jail there several times, helped to keep the temperature in Albany at boiling point.

It's not as if there weren't a lot of reporters converging on all these hot spots. The *New York Times*, in particular, had been blanketing the civil rights story, sending top-flight reporters such as Claude Sitton and Harrison Salisbury, who made sure that their readers, at least, were informed of the escalating crisis. Other journalists, like Robert E. Lee Baker of the *Washington Post*, John Herbers, who was based in Jackson for UPI, the trio of Karl Fleming, Bill Emerson, and Joe Cumming of *Newsweek*, David Halberstam of the *Nashville Tennessean*, John Chancellor and Sander Vanocur of NBC, and Harry Reasoner of CBS, all distinguished themselves and their news organizations with their reporting in the South. But the *Constitution*, which was consistently ranked among the nation's top ten newspapers in those days, mostly thanks to Ralph McGill, seldom covered events outside of Atlanta, using wire stories when a development was too big to ignore. Most papers in other parts of the South pretty much followed the same practice, except for the handful of progressive editors and publishers such as Harry Ashmore in Little Rock, Hodding Carter II (Big Hod) and his son Hodding Carter III of the Greenville, Mississippi, *Delta Democrat Times*, Hazel Brannon Smith, publisher of the *Lexington Advertiser*, and John Siegenthaler, editor and later publisher of the *Nashville Tennessean*.

While integration was stalled in the schools, neither had it advanced much in my profession. Whites held a near-total monopoly in the mainstream press; only a tiny handful of blacks served as reporters or editors at white-owned newspapers or broadcast outlets. At the *Constitution*, there was a single black newsman, Claude George, who wrote a weekly column entitled "Our Negro Community." He didn't have a desk in the newsroom but would walk in and deliver his column. That was pretty much the extent of the paper's coverage of the black community except for crime stories or racial unrest, or, occasionally, a black involved in sports or the entertainment world. If blacks wanted any other news about their race, they had to depend on the black-owned *Atlanta Daily World* or influential weeklies like *Jet* and *Ebony*.

By the midsixties, I was getting restless at the *Constitution*. I wanted a piece of the civil rights action. The story that best reflected the transformation of my views at the time—one of the last I covered for the *Atlanta Constitution*—was the murder of Lemuel Penn. Penn was a forty-nine-year-old U.S. Army Reserve officer and decorated World War II combat veteran who had just completed his annual tour of active duty at Fort Benning, Georgia. He was on his way back to Washington, DC, where he was assistant superintendant of schools, traveling with two other black reserve officers on July 11, 1964. They were riding in a Chevrolet Biscayne sedan. Penn was driving. As they passed through Athens, another car, a Chevy station wagon carrying three Klansmen, noticed the DC license plate on the Biscayne. According to testimony presented at the trial, one of the Klansmen, Howard Sims, said, "That must be one of President Johnson's boys. . . . I'm going to kill me a nigger."

Penn and his party evidently failed to notice the station wagon following them. When it pulled alongside them, Sims aimed his shotgun at Penn and pulled the trigger. So did Cecil Myers, who was in the back seat. Penn died instantly.

The more I learned about the murder, the more outraged I became. Although Athens city fathers expressed shock at the killing, I wrote a story stating that the town's climate of hate, fear, and intimidation practically guaranteed the death of innocents. As I knew from personal experience, the city had a history of turning its back on its uglier features. Four years earlier, when I exposed the whorehouses and big-time gambling operations that preyed on students, city and university officials set up howls of protest. It wasn't the criminal activity that infuriated them. They were denouncing me and the *Constitution* for reporting the truth. These civic leaders were equally incensed at the way the "outside" press had reported on the riot surrounding the integration of the University of Georgia in 1961.

Yet, for months before the Penn shooting, night-riding Klansmen had been terrorizing Negroes with impunity in Athens. Klansmen strutted around the streets at will, flogging and shooting Negroes. Motorcades of Klansmen invaded Negro neighborhoods and burned crosses on lawns. Out-of-state Negroes driving through Athens were frightened, cursed, and chased out of town—at least once in the presence of Athens policemen. Many violent incidents were never even reported. There were no arrests.

Klan activity had surged because local Negroes were demonstrating and picketing to end segregation in local businesses as required by the Civil Rights Act of 1964. The town's response was one of denial. Newspapers and radio station representatives met with merchants and agreed that racial demonstrations would be ignored. Most of the ministers in town seemed to agree with the argument that the more publicity, the more trouble it would cause. The outstanding exception was Father John J. Mulroy, pastor of the local Catholic church, who argued that Athenians should face their problems openly. Condemning the Klan in a sermon, he said they "came in the afternoon and they came in the evening. Some even wore holsters in which there were pistols. It was like being in Dodge City before Matt Dillon or even Chester came to town."

The trial of two of the Klansmen, which I covered, was a travesty. Everybody in that stifling courtroom knew it was a farce, and nobody knew it better than the black spectators seated in the Jim Crow balcony. The scene, which could have come straight out of *To Kill a Mockingbird*, became engraved in my memory, encapsulating as it did the terrible oppression of blacks in the South at that time.

For five days now a dozen Negroes had come to the Madison County Courthouse in Danielsville, Ga. (population 360). They climbed an outside stairway to the courtroom, stooped to avoid a low ceiling and stepped into a darkened Jim Crow balcony to watch the murder trial of two Ku Klux Klansmen.

Below them the Negroes could see the defendants, Howard Sims and Cecil Myers, smiling and waving at fellow Klansmen in the crowded, all-white section.

Outside, darkness began to fall and the Negroes showed signs of apprehension. Once in a while white faces turned upward to peer at the balcony. The black faces, leaning over the rail, withdrew quickly.

It was Sept. 4, 1964. The trial for the murder of Lemuel A.Penn, a Washington, D.C. public school official, was about to go to an all-white jury.

For five days the state had built an overwhelming case that the defendants, as part of a conspiracy to intimidate and kill Negroes, had ambushed Penn on the night of July 11, as he drove through Georgia en route to Washington after reserve officers' training at Ft. Benning, Ga.

In less than two hours the defense had presented its evidence. Sims and Myers spent less than 30 seconds each making unsworn statements (allowed under Georgia law with no cross-examination) denying they had killed Penn.

Regardless of the evidence, nobody—least of all the Negroes in the balcony—thought seriously that white men could be convicted of murdering a Negro in Madison County—not even if the victim happened to be a distinguished educator, a decorated combat veteran of World War II, a lieutenant colonel in the Army Reserves, and was just passing through.

In an hour-long racist argument, a defense attorney five times emphasized the Anglo-Saxon blood of the defendants and the jurors and shouted that FBI agents, on orders of President Johnson to "bring us white meat," had "infiltrated" Madison County. "Fe, Fi, Fo, Fum," the attorney shouted. "I smell the blood of an Englishman!"

The prosecutor cited the overwhelming evidence of guilt during the five-day trial and argued for a verdict "that will not be the ridicule of this country."

Darkness had fallen by the time the case went to the jury and fewer than 12 Negroes remained in the balcony. In groups of two and three they, too, began to slip down the stairway.

While waiting for the jury to return, I walked over to Howard Sims, a husky World War II navy veteran and avid gun collector who had been involved in Klan demonstrations and violence in several cities in Georgia, Florida, and Alabama. When I tried to interview him about his thoughts while the jury was determining his fate, he reacted angrily—not about my reporting of the Klan's part in killing Penn, but about my series on gambling in Athens. "You stink," he snarled. "You ruined the best part of Athens! You destroyed some of the finest social and service clubs in town. I wouldn't talk with you about anything."

When the jury returned and acquitted the two white men, the courtroom was packed with whites who cheered and applauded. But the balcony was empty. It was no time for a Negro to be anywhere near the courthouse.

Chapter 15

MAKING THE BREAK

BY THE TIME I FINISHED covering the Penn trial, I realized it was past time for me to start plunging into the civil rights movement and racism, that I was missing out on something huge and important. But the *Constitution* was not the place to start. Then, unexpectedly, the opportunity I needed came along.

A Nieman classmate of mine, David Kraslow, who was then with Knight Newspapers but later joined the *Los Angeles Times*, heard that the *Times* was planning to open a bureau in Atlanta in early 1965. He recommended me for the job. The voting rights drive in Selma, led by Martin Luther King Jr., was reaching a fever pitch, and I knew in my bones I had to be there, covering it. The *Constitution*, meanwhile, did not send a single reporter but stuck to its policy of using wire service stories.

Frank Haven, the *Times* managing editor, telephoned me to make an offer. Our conversation lasted no more than five minutes. He said he knew my record and wanted to hire me if I was interested and we could agree on a salary. The civil rights movement was not only dominating national news coverage but was getting attention worldwide—the principal reason, he said, that the *Times* was opening a southern bureau.

"What's your salary now?" asked Haven. "About $10,000 a year," I said. "We'll pay you $15,000," he said. There was no way I could turn it down.

When I broke the news to Gene Patterson, the *Constitution*'s executive editor (he was not yet writing the editorials for which he would become famous) he expressed astonishment at the size of the salary offer. He said the *Constitution* would hate to lose me and wondered if I couldn't remain at the paper, perhaps supplementing my salary with enough freelance assignments to equal the pay being offered by the *Times*. I have always admired Patterson greatly, and liked working for him, but I told him I had already accepted the *Times*' offer and that my decision was final.

Before either the *Times* or the *Constitution* could announce my appointment, I got a letter from my old boss, Cosmon Eisendrath, who had somehow found out about the *Times'* offer. I came across my reply to him recently, and I realize that my decision, which in retrospect looks like it should have been a slam-dunk, gave me pause at the time. As I wrote to him, a trifle grandiosely:

> I feel I'm making the right move (I know I am from a financial standpoint), but I leave the *Constitution* with great reluctance. No longer will I be so close to my stories. Nor will I be able to follow up specific subjects and help personally shape the course of human events. For example, the current session of the Legislature is acting in four different areas—legislative ethics, reform of Stone Mountain State Park operations, new mental health reforms, and marriage mills-- as a result of series I have written in the past year. I'm afraid my influence now will be so scattered and so dwarfed in a large, nationwide organization (even international with 10 foreign bureaus) that it will be hard to see at all.
>
> However, there are other compensations. My children now are ages 12 (Karen), 11 (Mike) and 10 (Steve) and next year Karen will be in high school—the eighth grade. Soon they'll all be ready for college and I'll need the wherewithal to send them.

My reluctance aside, I was feeling proud to be joining a newspaper with the reach and ambition of the *L.A. Times.* I have always been a great booster of any organization I've been associated with, and I have to laugh when I see how even before joining the *Times*, I was touting what a great paper it was. As I wrote to Mr. Eisendrath:

> . . . The *Times* is by far the nation's largest newspaper in advertising lineage with a total of about 89 million lines in 1963, compared to about 59 million for the No. 2 paper (*Miami Herald*). It is about third in daily circulation with more than 800,000. Sunday's circulation is second or third with 1,250,000.
>
> Although I will work directly for the *Los Angeles Times*, my copy will be available for distribution through the *Los Angeles Times–Washington Post* News Service, which services 43 American papers (including such large papers as the *New York Journal-American, Miami Herald, Detroit News, Charlotte Observer*, etc.), 11 Canadian papers, and 23 other foreign papers.

While those numbers are impressive, I did not mention that the *Times* was not then generally ranked among the best newspapers in the country despite recent improvements. "A few years back, it was a shoddy sheet of extreme right-wing viewpoint and a Hollywood divorce focus for its news measurement" is the way the *Economist* of London summed it up. But by 1965, it had improved dramatically, thanks to Otis Chandler, who succeeded his father, Norman, as publisher in 1960 and began taking immediate steps to strengthen the paper editorially.

For decades the *Times* had been a bastion of support for the wealthy and propertied, nurturing Republican politicians—the paper *made* Richard Nixon—and promoting conservative causes. It was considered such a right-wing rag that reporters in the tiny Washington bureau often could not get their phone calls to Democrats returned. The paper was also relentlessly local, so much so that one wit said a typical headline was "LA dog chases LA cat over LA fence." But Otis, a fiercely competitive man, wanted his paper to be nationally recognized for excellence, and he was prepared to spend the money needed to succeed—something he did in a remarkably short span of time. Establishing a new bureau to cover the turmoil in the South was a declaration of sorts. Aside from the wire services, the only other national outlets at the time with bureaus in the South that I can recall were the *New York Times*, *Newsweek*, and *Time* magazine. It was clearly a demonstration of how determined Otis was to take his place among the big boys.

The *Times* led by Otis was "a comet in ascent," wrote David Halberstam in *The Powers That Be*. "No publisher in America improved a paper so quickly on so grand a scale, took a paper that was marginal in its qualities and brought to it excellence, as Otis Chandler did."

Joining the *L.A. Times* opened up a whole new world for me in many ways. While I was no longer the biggest fish in the pond, it was exhilarating to be joining such a dynamic, nationally oriented publication. Even in Atlanta, I had become aware that the *L.A. Times* was a newspaper on the move. I was impressed when Bob Donovan, the much-admired bureau chief of the *New York Herald Tribune* and author of *PT 109: John F. Kennedy in WWII*, one of my favorite books, was hired to lead the *Times'* rapidly expanding Washington bureau. Under his leadership, the bureau was already becoming a force in town.

I was especially proud to be associated with Otis, whom I met not long after joining the paper. He was an amazing physical specimen, a six feet, three inch weightlifter with massive shoulders and a huge head topped by wavy golden hair. A former shot-putting champion, collector of vintage cars, serious race car driver, and big game hunter, he once shattered an ankle and broke several ribs in an encounter with a musk ox on an arctic hunting expedition. He was also an astute businessman whose various moves doubled the paper's circulation and sharply improved its bottom line.

Apart from being close in age, Otis and I didn't have much in common, but we got along well, I suppose because we were both absolutely dedicated to making the *Los Angeles Times* a great paper. Otis was a somewhat humorless man; you didn't have a lot of belly laughs with him. But he did make the occasional witty quip. One evening when he was in town, my wife, Barbara, and I joined him and Executive Editor Bill Thomas for drinks at a cocktail lounge featuring a piano player. After a time, Bill, an excellent musician, took a turn at the keyboard. Otis listened for a while and said, "The only thing I could do with that piano is lift it."

A year after I began working at the paper, I attended a *Times* awards banquet in Los Angeles where Otis spoke glowingly of the newspaper's progress and plans. Like the other employees, I cheered and applauded like mad when he said, "We're going to spend whatever it takes in money and manpower to make the *Los Angeles Times* the best newspaper in the country, and I mean better than the *New York Times*." As we would say in the South, I was in high cotton, and over the next decades I would see Chandler try to live up to that audacious promise.

Chapter 16

SELMA

I STARTED WITH the *Times* on February 1, 1965, but I scarcely had time to inspect my office and say hello to my new secretary before taking off for Selma. Dr. King's voting rights demonstrations, which began officially in January, were red hot, and Dallas County Sheriff Jim Clark and his deputies had already arrested about sixteen hundred demonstrators in the previous few days before I arrived.

I arrived with scant background on the situation, but Roy Reed, the Atlanta correspondent for the *New York Times*, gave me a complete fill on what had been going on, and what the major characters on both sides of the issue had been doing. Reed, who had just been recruited from the *Arkansas Gazette*, had been snapped up by the *Times* because he was a superb writer, and, like me, he "talked southern." I also got help from another outstanding *New York Times* reporter, Mississippian John Herbers.

Reporters from competing newspapers normally are highly competitive when covering the same story, of course. And I was somewhat surprised that reporters from a competing paper would so willingly cooperate with me on a story that was making headlines not only throughout the country, but throughout the world.

What I quickly realized was that because the story was breaking out in so many places at once and that reporters considered it so important to get it right, they were helping each other in almost unprecedented ways. In more than a half century of reporting, it was about the only time I experienced such wholesale joint efforts by reporters for rival publications covering a major running story. And they did it enthusiastically, wanting be sure that their competitors' readers would receive as full and accurate an accounting as their own readers.

The cooperation among competing media only extended to breaking news, of course. We all continued to write exclusive profiles, features, and investigative stories involving the civil rights movement. Inevitably, Roy and I became close friends and over the next few years continued to cooperate on other big, breaking civil rights stories. He, I, Gene Roberts, Karl Fleming, John Herbers, Bill Emerson of *Newsweek*, Arlie Schardt of *Time*, and others formed tight bonds akin to what happens to soldiers on the battlefield. We knew we were at the center of history-making events that would alter the political and social landscape of the South forever, and it was wildly exhilarating.

Not coincidentally, nearly all of us "regulars" were southerners. It was a huge advantage if you could "walk the walk and talk the talk." "Hey, what do you say, Calvin?" I'd greet Calvin Craig, Georgia's Grand Dragon of Shelton's United Klans of America, giving him a hearty handshake. "What's going on?" Craig, a longtime Klan leader, was always accessible to me by phone, letting me know when rallies were scheduled or some other Klan activity as long as it wasn't a covert operation.

My southern roots were helpful when I covered blacks as well, by whom I was seen as a kind of kindred soul. This was pointed up to me in Selma when Ray Rodgers, who was black, was sent down by the *Los Angeles Times* to join me. With his New York accent, natty wardrobe, and horn-rimmed glasses, Ray stuck out from most of the other assembled reporters. To the demonstrators he looked like an outsider, and they were reluctant to talk to him until I vouched for him.

When Reverend King decided to focus his efforts on Selma, the county seat of Dallas County, it was a shrewd tactical move. Selma had a history of entrenched white supremacy dating back to the early 1800s, when it was a center of slave trade for the cotton economy. At the time of the demonstrations, only about 355 of the town's 15,000 eligible blacks were registered to vote. Local blacks, joined by SNCC, the Student Nonviolent Coordinating Committee, had been demonstrating for two years in an attempt to increase their numbers. But their efforts had met with threats, arrests, and violence. One of the SNCC organizers, Bernard Lafayette, was beaten so badly he nearly died.

King was also attracted to Selma because of Jim Clark, its rabidly racist, made-for-TV sheriff. Clark's propensity for violence, King knew, could help mobilize public opinion nationwide to support voting rights—his number-one priority at that time. Clark certainly looked the part of the villain of the piece. Burly and tough-talking, he wore a gun on one hip, a night stick on the other and sometimes carried a cattle prod. He swaggered around with a lapel pin that said "Never"—his response to Negro demands to vote.

On one of my first days in Selma, Clark was in high dudgeon as he watched a King aide, the Reverend C. T. Vivian, a Baptist minister, try to enter the Dallas County Courthouse. Clark rushed toward Vivian, a slight, distinguished figure of a man, yelling to his deputies, "Get that nigger off the courthouse steps!"

Not waiting for the deputies, Clark rushed over and struck Vivian on the jaw, sending him staggering down the steps where the sheriff's deputies grabbed him, handcuffed him, and hustled him away to jail on a trumped-up contempt of court charge, all recorded by the network news cameras.

Clark, apparently, was totally oblivious to the way his actions played on TV. A few weeks earlier, he was filmed beating a fifty-four-year-old black woman, Annie Lee Cooper, who had been waiting on the steps of the courthouse to register to vote. The altercation started with Clark prodding the 225-pound woman in the neck with a billy club. She turned around and socked him as hard as she could, sending him flying backwards. His deputies then held her down, while Clark hit her again and again with his club. He later claimed that she had taken his club and he was just trying to get it back, but "those damn newspaper fellows made it look like I was beating her."

Several days after the Vivian episode, I interviewed Clark in his office, and the sheriff, grinning broadly, showed me a telegram from Tulsa, Oklahoma, that began, "Congratulations. Use your head. Don't waste your fist on a dumb nigger's jaw." The telegram was signed, "a Southerner at heart."

"There's a lot of truth in that," Clark told me, holding up his left hand to show a split and bandage on the ring finger. "You know I really don't remember hitting that nigger. But the bone in my finger is split."

At the time the *Los Angeles Times* had a ban on using the term "nigger" in its news columns. And after I dictated my story over the telephone to a machine in Los Angeles, I received a call from an editor on the national desk who informed me in no uncertain terms that "we can't use 'nigger' in our stories. The word's offensive and we're just not allowed to use it in the *Times.*"

"What are we gonna do," I practically shouted, "have Sheriff Clark saying, "Get those N-e-g-r-o-e-s off the courthouse steps? We can't do that! It wouldn't be true and it wouldn't convey the true meaning of what happened!" I told him I intended to argue the case to other editors if he insisted on Clark not being quoted accurately. He said he would check on it and get back to me.

He passed along my argument to senior editors and they agreed with me that it would destroy the tone and truth of the story if we didn't quote Clark accurately. Thereafter, any time the word "nigger" was used in such offensive ways by segregationists in a story I was covering—and there were many such times—I used it in quotes and the *Times* left it in.

(Many newspapers today still refuse to cite the word even in quotes and refer to it as "the 'n' word." Moreover, in 2007 the National Association for the Advancement of Colored People branded it an outlaw word never to be used. Nevertheless, it's a term deeply embedded in American history and literature, i.e., "Nigger Jim" in Mark Twain's *Tom Sawyer* and still voiced as a pejorative by many whites. And to say it shouldn't be used even in accurately quoting racists makes no sense to me nor to many reporters and editors I know, white and black.)

Clark was so proud of the many telegrams, letters, and other messages he received from throughout the country congratulating him for his fierce resistance to the demonstrations and for his assault on Vivian that he pointed out a number of them on a large bulletin board in his office.

"Keep up the good work," wired a Buffalo, New York, man. "If in need of steamroller to make black top let us know." A "thank God for a sheriff like you" telegram came from a man in Sidney Point, North Carolina, who referred to Dr. King as a "half-breed roaming from one state to another inciting riots." The Mississippi Sheriffs' Association sent a "deepest sympathy and good luck" message, and the president of the United Daughters of the Confederacy sent a telegram saying, "Keep up the Good Work and God bless you."

"Look at that," Clark told me. "Most of 'em like what I'm doing—about 70 percent of 'em—and the 30 percent that don't I don't give a damn about."

Alabama state troopers were as out of control as Jim Clark and his deputies. On February 18, 1965, not long after Clark punched Vivian, the minister told a crowded civil rights protest meeting in a church in the nearby town of Marian about the assault. After the session, several hundred angry demonstrators filed out of the church and began a nighttime protest march. Suddenly the streetlights went out and a group of white toughs, along with some state troopers, began beating the demonstrators.

As they scattered in fear, one of them, eighty-two-year-old Cager Lee, sought safety in a nearby café after being savagely beaten, but was found there by state troopers and beaten again. When his daughter, Viola Jackson, tried to intervene, she was beaten, too. Then, when her son, Jimmy Lee Jackson, sought to protect her, he was shot and beaten, then dragged outside where he collapsed. Jackson died in a hospital several days later, touching off widespread demonstrations.

In the wake of Jackson's death, King called for a massive protest march from Selma to Montgomery, the state capital, on March 7—what would come to be known as Bloody Sunday. He had been leading voting rights demonstrations in Selma since January, but he decided to push back the March 7 date and returned to Atlanta to attend church services that day. Most of the print media, including me, accompanied him, confident that there would be no action in Selma without his presence. We were wrong.

When several hundred people bent on marching turned up on the seventh at Brown's Chapel, headquarters of the protest movement, King's colleagues hurriedly decided they had better go ahead with the march after all. So I and a lot of my colleagues, who were in Atlanta with King, missed what was arguably the turning point of the entire civil rights movement: the sight of hundreds of state troopers and dozens of club-wielding sheriff's deputies, some on horseback, charging into a kneeling, praying group of protesters on the Edmund Pettus Bridge. To add to the horror of the scene, a mob of white citizens gathered to watch the confrontation, cheering and whooping. Fortunately for the movement, the television cameras were there, and they recorded the iconic images that would be shown again and again.

I drove back to Selma as fast as I could, and I didn't have to wait long for the next violent outbreak. Two days after Bloody Sunday, three out-of-town ministers were savagely beaten by a gang of whites as the trio emerged from a Negro-owned restaurant. One of them, James Reeb, a white Unitarian minister from Boston and member of King's Southern Christian Leadership Conference, was clubbed so severely he was taken to a hospital in Birmingham where he was not expected to live. I will never forget standing outside the hospital in a cold rain that night, surrounded by several hundred civil rights demonstrators who listened in mournful silence to the announcement of Reeb's death.

The minister's death kicked off an uproar across the nation. Thousands of people in places like Boston, New York, Flint, Michigan, and Louisville, Kentucky, took to the streets to show their sympathy with the civil rights drive in Selma. Hordes of others—priests, nuns, ministers, college students, and ordinary citizens—poured into Selma itself, all wanting "to do something." City officials, aghast at the negative publicity, authorized use of the municipally owned stadium for the Reeb memorial. At the national level, President Lyndon Johnson introduced a voting rights bill to a joint session of Congress on March 15, four days after Reeb died, appropriating the movement's own slogan, "We shall overcome."

While blacks expressed sympathy for the slain minister, some bitterly compared the reaction to his death to that of young Jimmy Lee Jackson, who had died a week earlier trying to protect his mother from being beaten by state troopers. I thought at the time and still do that the dissenters had a point. As Stokely Carmichael is reported to have said, "What you want is the nation to be upset when anybody is killed. But it almost seems that for this to be recognized, a white person must be killed."

Capitalizing on the outpouring of sympathy, Dr. King announced a new march from Selma to Montgomery for March 21. Along with hundreds of other journalists I covered that famous fifty-four-mile, five-day trek, which, under President Lyndon Johnson's orders, was heavily guarded by about two thousand soldiers, eighteen hundred National Guardsmen, one hundred FBI agents, and one hundred federal marshals. This time, nearly four thousand people gathered at Brown's Chapel to kick off the Selma leg, and the crowd swelled as it approached Montgomery. I was full of admiration for the bravery and endurance of the marchers, the majority of whom were black, although there was a sizeable number of whites who walked alongside them, all of them enduring harsh, chill rains alternating with blazing sunshine. (Oddly, I don't remember any physical discomfort of my own; I was too busy writing and reporting to notice the weather.) The march ended peacefully with Dr. King addressing a crowd of more than twenty-five thousand at the state capitol, but the peace would not last long.

That evening, after the crowd had dispersed, John Doar, the no-nonsense, straight-talking chief of the Justice Department's Civil Rights Division, sat at a table chatting with me and several others at the Elite Café, a hangout for journalists covering the civil rights story. While Doar usually chose his words carefully and talked guardedly with reporters, that night he was expansive, commenting on how peacefully everything had gone despite all the violence that had led up to the march. We were midway through the meal when he was paged for a telephone call.

He was ashen-faced when he retuned to the table. He told us he had just been notified that a white woman who had participated as a volunteer in the march had been shot to death. She was Mrs. Viola Liuzzo, a white housewife and mother of five from Detroit who had impulsively gone down to Selma to see if she could be of any help. She had been driving from Selma to Montgomery to ferry demonstrators back to Brown's Chapel when she was killed by shots fired from a car that pulled alongside her car. A passenger in her car, Leroy Molton, a young black civil rights worker, escaped injury. But Mrs. Liuzzo's death set off new clamors for legislation to guarantee voting rights for blacks.

In Washington President Johnson went on television within twenty-four hours to announce that the FBI had arrested four Ku Klux Klansmen and that they would be brought to trial on charges of murdering Mrs. Liuzzo. My antennae went up immediately when I heard how speedily the suspects had been arrested. Knowing that the FBI had heavily infiltrated the Klan, I was pretty sure a Klan informant had to be the key to such quick action. I began working my law enforcement sources, and it didn't take long to learn that the arrests were based on testimony by Gary Tommy Rowe Jr., an informant who was one of the four Klansmen in the car.

The result was a page-one story in the *Los Angeles Times* headlined "Liuzzo Slaying Figure Seen as FBI Informer." The story provoked little national reaction, as was often the case when the *L.A. Times* broke a story. But three days later the *New York Times* carried a page-one story with essentially the same facts and an almost identical headline, "Liuzzo Witness an FBI Informer." It was written by Fred Graham, a *New York Times* reporter who later became a close friend of mine, and it made front pages and television and radio news shows across the country. The wire services and electronic news media regularly monitored and quoted the *New York Times* in those days, but not the *Los Angeles Times*.

I was incensed and so were editors in Los Angeles that our Liuzzo story had been ignored while the *New York Times* story was being widely quoted. We complained so bitterly and frequently that our exclusives were being ignored that the wire services and electronic news media finally began taking notice of some of our exclusives and citing them in their reports—a battle I would continue to fight after I got to Washington and became the *Times*' bureau chief.

Congress passed the 1965 Voting Rights Act following the Selma-to-Montgomery march, and President Johnson signed it into law on August 6. (A few years later, Selma officials, seeking to improve the town's reputation, actually had the chutzpah to boast that it was the "birthplace of the Voting Rights Act.") The following year, however, Clark sought reelection and faced a strong challenge from Wilson Baker, Selma's public safety director. Baker, a moderate on racial issues, was a strong favorite among blacks and about eighty-five hundred more blacks had been registered under the new act. So Clark, hoping to attract some black support without alienating his segregationist base, held a barbecue on the outskirts of Selma for a number of influential blacks.

After finding out about Clark's ploy, I interviewed a number of blacks who favored Baker and monitored the barbecue. I wound up writing a story reporting there were more blacks in the bushes taking notes on who attended the barbecue than there were blacks in attendance. The story got big page-one play in the *Los Angeles Times* under a three-column headline: "Clark's Fat in the Fire over Selma Barbecue." And it was played around the country in newspapers that subscribed to the *Los Angeles Times/Washington Post* News Service. Several clippings of the stories were sent to folks in Selma, including the sheriff.

I reported that rumors of the barbecue had "brought guffaws from many Negroes and grumbles from white segregationists" who were already upset that Clark had stopped wearing the "Never" buttons he had sported to show his opposition to desegregation. And I pointed out that the barbecue and political rally for Clark were arranged by two brothers and quoted a local Negro as saying, "They're usually called 'Big 'Un' and 'Little 'Un,' but we just call 'em 'Jim Clark's niggers.'"

Blacks found my story hilarious. Clark found it infuriating. I quickly learned that when I encountered him as we approached each other walking down the corridor of the first floor in the Dallas County Courthouse. He was flanked by two hefty deputies and all three of them were glaring at me. I reached out for a handshake and said, "Hello, sheriff, how you doing?" Clark, clenching his fists and shaking in fury, practically shouted, "Why don't you go to hell, you lyin' son of a bitch!"

The deputies suddenly made a menacing move toward me. I didn't tarry. I quickly turned around and mounted the stairs to the second floor where a hearing was being held to verify Baker's election victory over Clark.

Minutes later Adam Clymer, then a reporter for the *Baltimore Sun*, came stumbling up the steps, gasping for breath and clutching his stomach. "What did you do, what did you to do to get Clark and his deputies so mad?" Clymer demanded.

Clymer had approached Clark and the deputies the same way I had and had no sooner greeted the sheriff than one of the deputies punched him. Clymer, later a long-time reporter for the *New York Times*, heard the deputy mutter something about "a no-good lyin' son of a bitch" before punching him.

Chapter 17

JIM CROW JUSTICE

I REMAINED HAUNTED by the Lemuel Penn trial, in which the all-white jury refused to convict the two Klansmen despite overwhelming evidence of their guilt. The outcome got me to thinking about how blacks were being grossly and systematically mistreated by the judicial system in the Deep South, and I started digging into the subject while still covering Selma. Now operating in high dudgeon mode, I collected enough information within four months to write a series of articles which ran in the *Times* on page one for five consecutive days under the headline "Jim Crow Justice."

My intention was to illustrate the cruel double standard that operated when it came to crime and punishment in the Deep South. I also wanted to show how the legal system, so often perverted to protect "the southern way of life," was integral to the perpetuation of segregation and oppression. To me, nothing illustrated this better than the black spectators who vanished from the balcony in Athens as the verdict was read in the Penn trial. As I noted when I recounted the scene in the *L.A. Times* series, the only time a Negro could afford to be seen in a courthouse was when he was there as a defendant, a witness, a floor sweeper, or a taxpayer.

I found the statistics on exclusion of blacks at every level of the process appalling. All 65 district federal judges in the 11 states of the old Confederacy were white. So were the 28 district clerks and all 109 jury commissioners. Of more than 1100 judicial officials in those states, fewer than 25 were Negro, and they were all lower-echelon employees.

Looking back over my series now, I am struck by the passion with which I wrote. The language I used would be considered over the top by the mainstream press today, though maybe not on cable TV news. I had clearly made the transition from passive, sympathetic observer to emotional participant. Like many reporters covering civil rights, I strongly

believed that there was but one side to the story when it came to segregation and I saw no need to pretend to be taking an objective stance.

"Nowhere is the degradation and oppression of the Negro more
abject than in some Jim Crow courthouses," I wrote in a piece headlined
"Reform Long Needed in U.S. Court System." "No matter how brutal the
killing, the chance of convicting a segregationist of killing a Negro or a
white integrationist is practically nil in many parts of the South."

Sadly, I had plenty of material to illustrate my point, including officials
like U.S. District Judge Harold Cox, who openly referred to Negroes as
"niggers" in his courtroom, saying they acted "like a bunch of chimpan-
zees." Cox was a petulant sort of racist. He was not amused when I quoted
the chimpanzee remark in a story for the *Los Angeles Times* while he
was presiding over the trial of Klansmen who killed the three civil rights
workers in Philadelphia, Mississippi. On Cox's orders, I was bounced out
of the courtroom's press section by a marshal who said, "The judge don't
like the way you quoted him and he don't want you to have the privilege
of the press section."

Judge Cox could be as insulting to whites he disliked as he was to
blacks. I recall the testy letter he sent to John Doar, the lead attorney of
the Justice Department's Civil Rights Division in the South in those days,
responding to Doar's request for a trial date for a voting rights case. Cox,
in a stinging reply, accused Doar of being "impudent" and "completely
stupid." And the judge declared, "I spend most of my time in fooling with
lousy cases brought before me by your department in the civil rights field."

If there was no shortage of villains to write about, there was no shortage of heroes, either. One was Charles (Chuck) Morgan Jr., a brilliant
Birmingham, Alabama, attorney who fought fiercely for the equality of
Negroes before the law. A good friend of mine, Chuck, along with my
professors at Harvard, greatly expanded my understanding of how race
and justice were intertwined. He was no mere observer. On September
16, 1963, a day after four Negro schoolgirls were killed in a Ku Klux Klan
bombing of a church in Birmingham, Morgan made a fiery speech before
a businessman's club blaming the city's white leaders for encouraging an
atmosphere of racism and violence that led to the bombing.

"Four little girls were killed in Birmingham yesterday," he said. "A
mad, remorseful, worried community asks, 'Who did it? Who threw that
bomb? Was it a Negro or a white?' The answer should be, 'We all did it.'"

The white community's reaction was swift and unforgiving. The death
threats to him and his family from violent extremists were so vicious and
so credible the Morgan family was forced to flee Birmingham by the

end of the week. They departed so hastily they had to leave behind the family dog. Chuck moved them to Atlanta where he became head of the American Civil Liberties Union's Southeastern Regional Office and continued to fight vigorously for racial equality and justice. He wrote a book about his experiences, *A Time to Speak*, and became one of the most valuable sources of my career—as well as a friend and a source for many other reporters.

It was Chuck who got me to write about Boaz Sanders, a client of his, a Negro indicted on a charge of murdering a white man in Birmingham, Alabama. In a motion to quash the indictment, Morgan repeatedly showed how a Negro defendant faced a system of justice entirely administered by whites.

His motion carried Sanders from arrest by white officers and transportation in a segregated paddy wagon driven by a white man to a segregated jail staffed entirely by whites to a courthouse of all-white officials and all-white jurors, where Negro spectators were segregated.

> If he receives the death penalty [the motion continued], he will then be given a last meal by his white guards, visited by a white chaplain, shaved by a white barber, and taken by white guards to a yellow electric chair in Kilby prison, the only facility in Alabama justice which is and has always been desegregated . . .
>
> A button or switch will be pressed by a white man before white witnesses, and the condemned man will die. Being in indigent circumstances, he will thereafter be buried in a potter's grave in a racially segregated cemetery provided by the State of Alabama.

Morgan, a heavyset, garrulous, pear-shaped individual who at one time consumed enormous quantities of vodka, was not afraid to speak the truth publicly. But he was a fairly prominent exception. Even under the cloak of anonymity, it took bravery to expose racial wrongs. I remember the state appellate court judge who was the source for several of the injustices I cited in the series asking not to be identified in any way, not even having his state identified. "It would be political suicide if I openly spoke that way," he said.

The judge's reaction reminded me of a story told to me by Selma newspaper editor Roswell Falkenberry, a gutsy journalist who wrote editorials critical of Sheriff Jim Clark and the way the demonstrators were handled. He got plenty of threats for his stance and zero public support. "I've had businessmen and others come up to me and whisper that they agree with me," he said. "But they don't want other people to know that's the way they feel."

Another invaluable source in the Jim Crow justice series was a conscience-stricken state official who offered to share the records of some fifty cases having to do with the trial, sentencing, or parole of blacks. But the official, a longtime source of mine, insisted that I come to his office at night. "Don't even identify the state," he said as he handed me a stack of records. "It's immaterial anyway. The same things happen in other states."

My source, I can now disclose, was Walter (Bee) Brooks, who was then chairman of the Georgia Pardon and Paroles Board and a long-time power in Georgia politics, mostly behind the scenes. While he was alive, I felt bound by his request to remain anonymous. But he died many years ago and his intentions, namely exposing blatant cases of injustice, were admirable. So I've felt free to identify him since his death.

Brooks made it clear he was appalled by the gross injustices he found while reviewing past records of criminal cases involving blacks that were brought before the Pardon and Paroles Board before he became chairman.

Sitting there with him, reviewing one miscarriage of justice after another, was both troubling and shocking. There was the case of the black teenager who had never been in trouble and who was hunting when a gang of white boys on a drinking binge came across him and decided to haze him. One of them grabbed his gun and it accidentally fired, killing the son of a leading citizen. An all-white jury convicted the boy of murder and sentenced him to life imprisonment. "If the boy had been white," a witness said, "he never would have been tried."

In another case, an elderly white woman, jaywalking despite being warned repeatedly by police, was killed when she walked into the side of a car driven by a Negro. After pressure by the woman's relatives, the Negro was charged with manslaughter. Rather than face an all-white jury, the defendant pleaded guilty and received a five-year sentence. A local police officer called it a "raw deal" and said the woman's death "was strictly accidental."

As Brooks explained, Negroes were so fearful of the courts that even in cases where they were innocent, they often gambled with a guilty plea in hopes a white judge would show more mercy than a white jury. But such hopes were often dashed. He cited the case of a Negro who pleaded guilty to charges involving two minor burglaries and received two fifteen-year sentences to run concurrently. As he was leaving the courtroom, the defendant muttered that the judge "really stuck it to me." The judge overheard the remark and ordered that the sentences run consecutively, doubling the man's prison time.

One pattern that jumped out was how harshly black teenagers were treated. A young man with no previous arrests had left his state looking for a job. Hungry and penniless, he broke into a small grocery and was eating Vienna sausage from a can when local police caught him. He received five years for burglary.

Negroes involved in traffic accidents involving white fatalities could expect the worst. "You get a Negro drinking and driving and if there's a white fatality, he's in real trouble—murder or manslaughter," said Brooks. "If it's a white driver, nothing's done in most cases. It's sort of like the electric chair, an honor reserved for a favored few—Negroes and maybe poor whites."

Race was a deciding factors in many a murder case as well. The fact is that in those days, a white man simply wouldn't be convicted of murder, no matter how heinous the crime, if the victim was a Negro. When one Negro murdered another, it often came down to whether or not he was considered a "good" Negro or not. Chuck Morgan, who defended many Negroes while still practicing law in Birmingham, used that mindset to his clients' advantage.

"The best defense in a southern court when you have a Negro client charged with murdering another Negro is to bring in the client's white employer and have him testify, 'He's a good nigger, honest and does his job,'" Chuck told me.

My series did not confine its targets to racist judges and all-white juries but took aim at the Justice Department as well. I pointed out that despite systematic exclusion, the department had yet to prosecute any official in the country for flouting an 1875 law that made it a crime to discriminate when picking juries.

Yet the Negro was not friendless at the federal level. One place where he could hope to get justice was before the U.S. Court of Appeals for the Fifth Circuit, covering a swath from Florida to Texas and led by the great jurist Elbert Tuttle. Backed by fellow progressives on the bench, Tuttle issued a series of momentous rulings such as permitting Martin Luther King Jr. to conduct demonstrations in Albany, Georgia, and ruling that James Meredith could be admitted to the University of Mississippi.

Tuttle may never have become a household name, but to reporters like me who covered civil rights, he was a giant. If I had my way, every student in America would be required to read *Unlikely Heroes: The Dramatic Story of the Southern Judges of the Fifth Circuit Who Translated the Supreme Court's Brown Decision into a Revolution for Equality*, written by my friend and colleague Jack Bass.

Physical bravery was not in short supply in those days either. The young Freedom Riders, students such as Charlayne Hunter and Hamilton Holmes, who braved mobs to enroll in the University of Georgia, the SNCC workers trying to register blacks in lonely, rural areas, risking injury, even death—how could you not admire them? There's place in that pantheon, too, for white attorneys like Al Bronstein, with the Lawyers' Constitutional Defense Committee, who would walk into threatening Mississippi jails late at night, all five feet, six inches of him, and post bail for young demonstrators.

Another man who loomed large in the struggle for equal justice for blacks was the Justice Department's John Doar, the federal government's point man in the South during those tumultuous years. A reserved, six-foot, two-inch Princeton graduate who reminded a lot of people of Jimmy Stewart, Doar was fearless, whether he was escorting James Meredith in his attempts to register at Ole Miss or walking alongside the marchers from Selma to Montgomery. His most mythic achievement came in the midst of a near-riot in Jackson, Mississippi, the day of Medgar Evers's funeral. As Jackson police stood shoulder to shoulder in the broiling heat, pistols drawn, trying to halt an impromptu demonstration, hundreds of angry blacks kept advancing towards them. Suddenly Doar, a lone figure in white shirtsleeves, walked out into the middle of the street where the two sides were facing off against each other. "My name is John Doar," he said, "D-O-A-R" and proceeded to persuade the demonstrators to disperse peacefully before they were mowed down.

Doar was a lifeline to reporters. In that extraordinary cauldron in which we were operating, we willingly, even eagerly, broke the newsman's tradition of trying to keep an arm's-length distance from government officials we were covering. This was especially true of our relationship to the attorneys in the Justice Department's Civil Rights Division. Normally, government attorneys are circumspect in dealing with reporters, but the division attorneys viewed the press as a valuable ally in curbing lawlessness and injustices, and they rightly saw us as an asset in building national support for their efforts.

Their cooperation with us sometimes went so far as to include disclosing information they might normally consider confidential. We, in turn, traded leads and tips with the attorneys. The lawyers also earned the gratitude of journalists who felt safer just knowing they were around when violence was threatening.

My good friend Arlie Schardt might not be with us today if it hadn't been for Doar. Arlie was covering the James Meredith March Against Fear in Mississippi in 1966 for *Time* magazine when he broke off from the march to interview some sharecroppers at a plantation. As he sat on a porch talking with them, two Neshoba County sheriff's deputies drove up and accused him of trespassing. They ordered him into their car and told him they were taking him to the Neshoba jail in Philadelphia, by then an infamous place.

Schardt had covered the story of the three civil rights workers whose bullet-ridden bodies had been found in an earthen dam after Neshoba County deputies had slapped them in the very same county jail. Schardt later confessed to me that he was scared to death.

Then, playing out like a scene from a movie, John Doar, who was accompanying the Meredith march, came striding down the highway. The deputies pulled their car over to the side of the road to let the marchers pass, and Arlie saw his chance. He rolled down his window and hollered, "John, John." Doar walked over and asked, "Arlie, what are you doing in there?" Schardt explained the situation and said the deputies were taking him to jail. Doar leaned into the window of the front seat, and demanded with a knowing smile, "You fellas don't really want to do this, do you?"

"Oh, no sir. We just wanted to get him off the property," one of the deputies said, and he opened the door. Schardt jumped out and speedily walked away with Doar, counting himself one lucky son of a gun.

I have always thought that Doar and his fellow attorneys in the Civil Rights Division did not get enough credit for the profound impact they had on the South and the nation as a whole. Their duties—investigating civil rights violations, collecting information about discrimination, and submitting reports and recommendations to the president and Congress—played a major role in getting Congress to pass the 1964 Civil Rights Act and the 1965 Voting Rights Act.

The attorneys were also responsible for making sure that at least some racially motivated murders were punished, using the federal courts to prosecute previously acquitted defendants. The charge they used was conspiracy to deprive people of their civil rights. (Only state courts could bring murder charges.) After covering numerous trials like the Liuzzo case and the Reeb murder, where the defendants walked free, I was elated at the verdict in the second Liuzzo trial, when a jury in Montgomery found the three Klansmen guilty. Judge Frank Johnson, another great southern jurist, gave all three the maximum sentence of ten years. It may not have been the end of Jim Crow justice, but a mighty blow had been struck all the same.

Chapter 18

THE MEANEST TOWN IN THE SOUTH

THROUGHOUT MY LONG CAREER, I covered an untold number of scandals in Georgia, six presidential campaigns, the Watergate scandal and Nixon impeachment proceedings, and almost every major news development in Washington. But reporting on the South in the 1960s, when I finally applied my investigative experience to the unfolding drama of racial change, remains the most satisfying assignment of all.

I've talked about some of the heroes. I also encountered hundreds of vicious racists in different towns in the three states where I grew up and worked as a reporter—Alabama, Mississippi, and Georgia. But I found Bogalusa, Louisiana, to be the meanest, most racist town I had ever covered. This despite the boast by its chamber of commerce that Bogalusa was the "pearl" of the Pearl River Valley, "a friendly city and a center of farms, forests and factories."

At least one city police official agreed with my negative assessment. "You wanna know why Bogalusa's so mean?" he said on a not-for-attribution basis. "It's because it grew up around the world's largest sawmill. Ever hear of a sawmill town that wasn't mean?"

Bogalusa got its name from a creek which divides the city, flowing by and picking up waste from the mammoth Crown-Zellerbach industrial complex. At the time, the company was operating a huge paper mill, two chemical plants and nylon industries. The Bogalusa plant was a highly profitable operation for Crown-Zellerbach, but the paper mill belched acrid, sulfurous fumes from many stacks around the clock, a smelly, seven-day-a-week operation. While covering Bogalusa I stayed in a motel where the acrid smell permeated the rooms and made sleeping nearly impossible and uncomfortable at best.

When I commented to a visiting Crown-Zellerbach official from San Francisco that "the odor is enough to make Bogalusa mean," he replied, "Maybe so, but it is known as the million dollar smell."

The town had a population of twenty-three thousand that included many racists who supported violence against blacks, especially those demanding their civil rights. When blacks marched and demanded better job opportunities and other desegregation goals, even some supposedly dignified businessmen turned out to yell "nigger" and joined increasing talk that violence might be the only way to "keep the nigger in his place." Some of those very businessmen were members of the Ku Klux Klan.

When blacks were demonstrating during some of the hottest, most humid days in the summer of 1965, with temperatures soaring into the high nineties, I watched white women, sometimes numbering more than a hundred, roaming the streets waving Confederate flags and shrieking, "nigger, nigger." Mothers with babies in their arms and others with children watching from hoods of cars would scream epithets and work themselves into a frenzy over the sight of young white female demonstrators from the North holding hands with Negro boys. White toughs cruised the streets in scores of cars flying Confederate flags from windows or radio antennas.

While my reporting of such events stuck to the plain, unvarnished truth, the facts were so vivid and my writing so freewheeling that when I review some of my stories I wonder if there are editors today who might consider the facts too incendiary to be published. For example, consider this paragraph: "The depth and intensity of the hate of Bogalusa is seen in the snarls of white boys no older than 8 or 9, some egged on by their screeching mothers, but others apparently unaccompanied by adults. The hate is seen in the huge crowds—up to 2,000—attracted to racist rallies conducted by fanatics who preach violence and classify Negroes as 'inhuman, somewhere between a white man and an ape.'"

I saw rocks, bottles, and other objects rain down on civil rights marchers, injuring some of the demonstrators, while police officers usually did nothing to stop the attacks. Occasionally reporters covering the demonstrations got hit. Once a large rock hit me in the chest as I walked alongside a column of demonstrators. A notebook, cut off almost in half and concealed inside my coat pocket, cushioned the blow and kept me from being seriously injured.

Most reporters covering civil rights carried similar cut-off notebooks. They were what we all called the "Claude Sitton notebook," named after the famous trail-blazing *New York Times* civil rights reporter. Sitton began cutting his notebooks down to half-size so they could be concealed in his coat pockets to prevent the more violent hatemongers from recognizing him as a reporter when he covered demonstrations. And all of us wore coats and ties even on the hottest days and while walking alongside civil rights marches. We dressed that way not only because that's what reporters did in those days, but because we figured we might escape the wrath of marauding citizens by blending in with FBI agents and government attorneys monitoring the demonstrations.

One racist I saw attack demonstrators repeatedly was a husky twenty-one-year-old nightclub bouncer named Milton Parker. I was keeping my eye on him as he clenched his fists and stalked up and down Bogalusa's streets hitting demonstrators with virtual impunity while policemen looked the other way. But finally Bernard Williams, a big, tough, no-nonsense policeman who had just appeared on the scene, stopped Parker dead in his tracks as he rushed up and tried to throw a large metal bolt at James Farmer, head of the Congress of Racial Equality, who was leading a protest march.

In a lightning-like move, Williams grabbed Parker's arm as he pulled it back to throw the bolt, then held him in a headlock and pulled him into the back seat of a Bogalusa police car that whisked him away. Parker later was booked on two assault warrants. But he was not done with violence. I would encounter him later as he stalked me and other reporters covering a Klan rally near Crossroads, Mississippi, just across the Pearl River from Bogalusa.

Despite the arrest of Parker, racists continued to assault demonstrators at will until finally the U.S. Justice Department filed a civil court complaint that resulted in a federal court order holding Bogalusa police officials in contempt for failing to protect demonstrators and in some cases for joining in beating them. One of those held in contempt was Claxton Knight, Bogalusa's tough-talking police chief.

Knight's face was twisted in rage when I encountered him just outside federal court in New Orleans where Judge Herbert W. Christenberry had held him in contempt of court for failing to obey an earlier order to protect demonstrators. Knight thrust the clipping of a newspaper article in my face. It was my article about Bogalusa's meanness that had appeared not only in the *Los Angeles Times*, but in many newspapers around the country that subscribed to the *Los Angeles Times/Washington Post* News Service. And somebody had sent clippings of the story to Knight and several other people in Bogalusa.

"Did you write that?!" Knight demanded as he waved the clipping back and forth before thrusting it under my face.

I took the article and looked at it. My byline was prominently displayed under a headline branding Bogalusa as being mean because it grew up around the world's largest sawmill. "Yes," I told him. "My name is on it, isn't it?"

"Well, I'll tell you one goddam thing," he snarled, "people in Bogalusa have seen it, too, and they don't like it a goddam bit! You better keep your ass out of Bogalusa."

Despite his warning, I continued, with some caution and apprehension, to cover Bogalusa, including the case of Ku Klux Klansmen in a pickup truck who fired shotguns and killed a thirty-four-year-old black deputy sheriff and seriously wounded another one in nearby Varnado. The deputies were attacked even though neither was involved in the civil rights movement and both had been recently hired to work only in black areas of the county and weren't authorized to handle cases involving whites.

After Chief Deputy Sheriff Doyle Holiday, another no-nonsense law enforcement officer like Officer Bernard Williams, began investigating the shootings, he and his wife narrowly missed being injured or killed when racists fired repeatedly into their house while they were watching television one night. Holiday later told me, "They haven't scared anybody if that's what they were trying to do. They just made somebody real mad."

When I asked Sheriff Dorman Crowe about the incident he was beside himself with fury at the attack on his chief deputy. He attributed the shooting to "a bunch of half-wit kids." Although he failed to track down the "half-wit kids" and arrest them, he told me, "You'd perform a service by printing this as a warning to their parents. I'm afraid we're going to have some real trouble around here when one of the officers blows a kid's head off.

"They're the kids of some of these people who think the Communists are taking over the country. They've got junior branches of their organizations. We know who some of these children are and what their positions are in the organizations. Their parents actually believe in their hearts and so teach their children that if it wasn't for them, the Communists would take over at 12 o'clock."

Bogalusa's almost daily protest marches of several hundred blacks during the summer of 1965 often encountered counterdemonstrations by a small, scraggly group of whites led by two kooky rabble-rousers I had monitored for some time—J. B. Stoner, a Klansman from Atlanta who headed the so-called National States' Rights Party, a right-wing hate organization, and his colleague, the Rev. Connie Lynch of San Bernardino, California, who billed himself as the pastor of the Church of Jesus Christ, Incorporated. Both of them, with small Confederate flags protruding from their pockets, marched in front of their ragtag followers babbling, "Niggers, coons, jigaboos."

Stoner and Lynch worked up a crowd of several hundred whites in hate-mongering speeches that urged them to fire any black employees and try to force them out of the South. "The National States' Rights Party," Stoner declared, "does not preach nonviolence. We don't believe in tolerance. We don't believe in getting along with our enemy, and the nigger is our enemy."

One day during the Bogalusa demonstrations a man who identified himself as Richard Helms of New Orleans, the grand klaxon or public relations official of the Original Knights of the Ku Klux Klan, approached me and several other reporters and told us we should cover a Klan rally the next evening in Crossroads, Mississippi, just across the Pearl River from Bogalusa. It was going to be a huge rally, he said, and we were welcome to come and report on it. He volunteered that there wouldn't be any trouble and we wouldn't have to worry about our own safety because the Klan had plenty of security guards to look out for us.

I was among about a dozen reporters and members of two television crews who went to cover the Klan rally, acting as a kind of tour guide to out-of-towners, as I often did. The rally was held in a huge cow pasture with the speakers' platform mounted on the back of a large flatbed truck. The main lights came from television strobe lights. Most of the thousand or more Klansmen attending the rally were in overalls, blue jeans, or other work clothes with only a few dozen wearing robes and hoods.

We were met there by Richard Helms and once again he assured us there would be no trouble. All of us reporters and television crew members were dressed in coats and ties as usual and we drew suspicious glances from most of the crowd. Some Klansmen were menacing, frowning and muttering remarks about "the nigger lovin' press" and the "lyin' reporters."

The rally began on an unnerving note when Saxon Farmer, a Bogalusa oil distributor who helped arrange the rally, opened the program by calling for those armed with guns to turn them in to the Klan's own white-robed security guards—the only ones he said were authorized to be armed. It became even more unnerving when no one turned in any arms.

Speaker after speaker worked up the crowd with warnings that "the niggers and the Jews and the Communists" were trying to take over the world. Farmer hailed Bogalusa as "the white man's last stronghold." Speaking, he said, for the great majority of whites at the rally, he wanted it known his brand of Jim Crow was branded in Bogalusa whites from birth. "I was holding my grandbaby in my arms the other day," he said, "and thinking, 'This is the littlest rebel in Bogalusa.'"

That brought raucous laughter and boisterous cheers from the crowd. But as other speakers followed and the hate-mongering continued, we reporters, who had stayed close to each other near the flatbed truck, were becoming uneasy and discussed whether we should leave before the rally ended. I felt we should leave because I had heard some of the Klansmen muttering that we had better get the hell out of there before we got the hell beat out of us.

My fellow reporters, including my friend Gene Roberts Jr., Nicholas Von Hoffman of the *Chicago Daily News*, and the nattily clad Richard Harkness of *NBC News*, who with his monogrammed handkerchief in his coat pocket looked for all the world like the fastidious film star Adolphe Menjou, quickly agreed we should leave immediately. But a young New Orleans *Times-Picayune* reporter who lived nearby said he was well acquainted with Saxon Farmer and suggested we wait until he could check with Farmer about providing us with protection while we walked to the part of the field where our cars were parked.

We agreed, and he walked over to talk to Farmer. He returned moments later, his face as white as the Klansmen's robes, and in a trembling voice said, "He says he can't do anything for us now, he's too busy, wait 'til the end of the rally."

None of us thought it was a good idea to wait until the rally ended, so we began walking toward our cars about a hundred yards away. I was leading us through the crowd when suddenly out of the corner of my eye I spotted Milton Parker off to the side, accompanied by several other toughs, obviously stalking us, and it looked like they were carrying clubs and pipes. I stopped suddenly and, without looking around, told Gene and the other reporters, "Don't say anything and don't look around. Just turn around and go back to the speakers' platform." They all followed my advice and we hurriedly walked back to the flatbed truck.

I looked around and finally spotted Richard Helms, the Klan's public relations guy. I rushed over to him, pointed my finger under his nose and said, "You said there wasn't going to be any trouble, didn't you?"

"Yes, I said there wouldn't be any trouble," he said.

"You said you wanted us here so you could get some good publicity, right?"

"Right."

"Well, you're about to get some bad publicity. That crowd's about to kick our asses, and if it does, you ain't gonna want to read the *Los Angeles Times* tomorrow."

Helms spoke into his walkie-talkie and ordered, "Get me a couple of armed men over here."

"A couple won't do it," I said, as several hard-eyed Klansmen jostled around us, fixing us with menacing looks.

"Change that," Helms said into his walkie-talkie. "Get me a dozen men. Make it a wedge. I want a flying wedge."

Minutes later a dozen robed Klansmen, all with pistols drawn, assembled a V-shaped formation around about an equal number of us reporters and escorted us through the booing and hissing Klansmen to our cars. We hightailed it out of there, figuring we were lucky to escape without being beaten or worse.

Bogalusa was such a racial tinderbox and hotbed of Ku Klux Klansmen that the mayor, Jesse H. Cutrer Jr., accompanied by Arnold Spiers, the city's police commissioner, attended a meeting of about 150 hooded Klansmen at the city's Disabled American Veterans Hall to urge them to cancel a planned demonstration. The Klan had announced it would hold a mass meeting to protest a visit to Bogalusa by a former Arkansas congressman, Brooks Hays, a moderate on race who was despised by the Klan. The city officials persuaded the Klan to call off the protest, but the publicity about its plan prompted Hays to cancel his visit.

Cutrer and Spiers made no bones about their fear of the Klan when I interviewed them and later when they testified before a federal court in New Orleans hearing a petition to forbid the Klan from resorting to violence and intimidation in Bogalusa. No wonder they were fearful. The Bogalusa city attorney as well as several members of the city's auxiliary police force who monitored civil rights demonstrations turned out to be members of the Klan.

Cutrer said that at the Klan meeting, "It was just like being in a tomb. You're mighty right I was scared—scared to death . . . Everybody wore masks and nobody said anything. There was a pistol—a big old .45—and an ammunition belt and Bible on the table. I moved the pistol and pulled the Bible up in front of me and made them bow their heads in prayer with me. I told them, 'The Lord knows what's in your heart and I know what's in mine.' Then we said our little pieces and left. We talked rough, too. It must have had some effect because the next day they voted not to have the protest meeting."

I asked Spiers if he was frightened at the Klan meeting, too, and he said, "You damn right. We walked in there and I said something like, 'Hello, fellows,' and nobody said a damn thing. Nobody even nodded their heads."

Chapter 19

DEACONS FOR DEFENSE AND JUSTICE

IN BERT'S BARBERSHOP in what whites called Bogalusa's "Nigger-town," Charles Sims, the tough-talking head of the city's heavily armed Deacons for Defense and Justice, a black vigilante group, told me how he had been threatened by white racists while picketing for civil rights on a downtown street.

"They said, 'Nigger, we're gonna getcha.' I said, 'You better steal me, 'cause you better not let me see you.'"

Along the wall of the one-chair barbershop, several sullen-faced young blacks slouched in chairs and watched intently as I interviewed Sims, a chunky but muscular man who deemed himself ready and eager to strike back if the racists wanted to strike the first blow. Smiling wryly, he exposed several gaps in his teeth. "The Deacons," he assured me, "was organized because we wasn't gettin' police protection. We organized for defense."

The Deacons for Defense and Justice had been formed several months earlier, in November 1964, in nearby Jonesboro to help protect civil rights demonstrators from Ku Klux Klan violence. And Sims was one of several blacks who formed it after the civil rights struggle heated up in Bogalusa. The blacks acted after concluding they could not count on state or local police to protect the civil rights demonstrators.

I had never before heard of a black vigilante group, although it turned out that there were other groups of armed blacks elsewhere in the South. I asked Sims whether some folks might be afraid to be identified as Deacons for fear of incurring violence by the Klan and other racists. Before he could answer, Royan Burris, a thin young barber trimming a teenager's hair, whirled around and interjected, "I'm a Deacon and I'd be proud to be identified." In fact, all of the barbershop customers shook their heads in agreement. "We got guns, too," one of them said, "so let 'em come on."

As the customers talked, about fifteen black teenagers, some carrying homemade picket signs with such slogans as "Jim Crow Must Go" and "Give Us Jobs and We'll Give You Business," burst into the barbershop. One of the youths said, "One of them policemen told us, 'I've told you one of you niggers was gonna get it.' I guess he was talking about the deputy that got killed. One of 'em called me a black son of a bitch."

Sims suddenly bounded out of his chair with such force that he startled the youth as well as me and several others in the barbershop. "Who said that to you?" he shouted. "What's his badge number?"

"Number 5," the youth said. Another youth, wearing a straw hat emblazoned with "Freedom, freedom" on the band, ambled into the shop and upon seeing Sims quickly dropped his eyes.

"What's the matter with you?!" Sims demanded. "How come you ain't out picketin'?"

The boy protested that he had intended to picket, but Sims cut him off. "They whipped you. Eh? And I believe they scared you."

"Was he hurt when the whites attacked the picket line?" I asked Sims. Before he could answer, the youth removed his hat to show about three large wounds with stitches. Then, on orders from Sims, he left to "find badge number 5 and see who he is."

I asked Sims, a husky forty-two-year-old insurance agent who served as an army sergeant in Europe in World War II, about reports I had heard that he carried an automatic .30 caliber carbine in his car and usually packed a .38 pistol under his shirt. "I carry all kind of weapons," he said, smiling broadly, "but I can't talk about the Deacons and the number of weapons they carry 'cause it's none of your business."

He wasn't being hostile, he hastened to explain, but wanted me to know he wasn't interested in telling a reporter anything about the Deacons' weapons because he thought it helped the Deacons from a psychological standpoint to keep both the police and the Ku Klux Klan in the dark about the size of their arsenal.

I left the barbershop and drove several blocks to the home of another Deacons official, Robert Hicks, a thirty-six-year-old employee at the Crown-Zellerbach paper mill. It was a hot, humid afternoon with the temperature soaring above a hundred degrees—hot enough for the asphalt on the street in front of Hicks's small white frame house to melt in places and cling to the bottoms of shoes. As I approached the house, I suddenly saw a tall, trim but muscular black man, shirtless, his eyes closed, leaning back as though dozing in a chaise lounge. On his stomach lay an automatic pistol.

Approaching cautiously, I shouted, "Mr. Hicks, Mr. Hicks, I'm a reporter from the *Los Angeles Times* and I just want to interview you."

Suddenly his eyes opened and he leaned forward, his hand gripping the pistol. I froze in place as he raised the pistol and slowly looked me up and down. Finally, he lowered the pistol and said, "You say you a reporter? Okay, come on up. Can't be too careful these days."

Unlike Charles Sims, Hicks was amazingly open and soft-spoken, and he talked freely when I asked about the Deacons. "I'm a member and I guess we got 175 to 200 members in Bogalusa," he said. "We're armed—some automatic weapons and some other weapons—but only for self-defense."

Hicks was president of the Bogalusa Civic and Voters League, a civil rights group. And his house served as local headquarters for the national Congress of Racial Equality, which had been leading demonstrations protesting discrimination in employment. Already he had carried out the Deacons' vow to fire back at any whites who attacked homes of blacks.

A car full of whites had recently fired shots into his house and as the car raced away he had run outside with his gun and fired several shots at it. He felt sure he had hit the car, but didn't know whether anyone had been injured. "We want to be nonviolent," Hicks said, "but we don't want any monkey business around our homes."

The FBI branded the Deacons an extremist organization, but the Deacons pretty well lived up to their vow of being defensive and serving as armed guards to protect civil rights demonstrators. An FBI memo described them as "a gun carrying black vigilante group formed in Bogalusa, Louisiana, ostensibly for defensive purposes in retaliation for Klan acts against Negroes. It has membership of several hundred located primarily in Louisiana communities."

In the end, the demonstrators protected by the Deacons won several concessions, such as the hiring of black policemen and installing of streetlights in black neighborhoods. But more important, they forced the Justice Department to address Bogalusa's racial injustices and increase federal actions that ultimately desegregated public schools and broke down racial barriers in places of public accommodation.

The Deacons never took root outside of Louisiana and petered out after about three years, but the organization retains its place in history as one of the few black vigilante groups to challenge the Klan and other racist groups in the South.

Chapter 20

THE ORANGEBURG MASSACRE

ON FEBUARY 8, 1968, I was in Los Angeles visiting *Times* editors when a news bulletin came over the Associated Press wire reporting that at least three students had been killed and more than twenty injured in an "exchange of gunfire" with state troopers during a civil rights protest at the all-black South Carolina State College in Orangeburg. I told Ed Guthman it made no sense to me that a group of students would be so foolish as to engage in a gun battle with heavily armed state troopers. He agreed and I immediately flew to South Carolina to check out the story.

Governor Robert E. McNair had already defended the state troopers' action as necessary to protect life and property. He charged that students at the college, who had built a bonfire on a street in front of the campus, had hurled missiles at the troopers and exchanged gunfire with them. He also accused the students of hurling at least two Molotov cocktails, one starting a fire at a warehouse not far from the campus.

Arriving in Orangeburg, I drove immediately to the Orangeburg Regional Hospital where twenty-seven wounded students were being treated. I walked into the office of Phil Mabry, the hospital's administrator, shook hands with him, identified myself as being from the Atlanta bureau, and in a businesslike manner, said I was there to examine the medical records of the wounded students. He said he would like to help if he could.

The Atlanta bureau I mentioned was of course an office of the *Los Angeles Times*, but the way Mabry quickly offered to help, he probably thought I was talking about the Atlanta office of the FBI, and I didn't disabuse him of that notion. In any event, he did mention there were privacy laws concerning disclosing the names of hospital patients. I told him I didn't want to see their names, they could be blocked out, but it was important for me to see where the students had been wounded.

Mabry then brought out records on the students who had been shot, spread them out on a desk and used a piece of paper to block out their names before letting me examine them. I hurriedly scribbled notes of records that indicated most of the students who were killed or injured had been caught in a deadly crossfire as they were running away from the troopers on their own campus. At least sixteen were struck from the rear. Two of the three who were fatally injured were shot in the back. A number of the students were on the ground when shot, some crawling, others lying flat. Some got up and ran and were shot a second time. Two were shot in the soles of their feet. They were all hit by deadly buckshot.

Armed with that evidence I began looking into the allegations of an "exchange of gunfire," which continued to be repeated in news accounts, although civil rights leaders were already describing it as a "massacre." None of the state patrolmen had been shot and they had confiscated no weapons from students. No one reported seeing any students with fire-arms. I found some witnesses who said that fifteen or twenty minutes before the police barrage, they thought they heard some shots being fired on the state college campus and on the adjoining campus of Claflin College, also predominantly black. But there were no reports of anyone being hit by gunfire, and officials cited no evidence of any students being armed.

Several students told me that one of those killed, Henry Smith, an eighteen-year-old sophomore who was shot in the right side and the left side of his neck, was dragged off campus by troopers who continued to strike him with a gun butt and billy clubs after he was shot. One of the students told me that Smith, just before he died, gasped, "You can hit me, but you can't hurt me no more."

From eyewitness accounts and official records, I concluded that when the shooting broke out there were about a hundred students milling around on campus at the top of an eight-foot embankment and they were confronted by forty state troopers armed with shotguns and automatic weapons and backed up by about forty-five National Guardsmen. Several city policemen were also on the scene, meaning that essentially there was at least one armed officer for every student. In addition, sixty-one other state patrolmen and three hundred ninety-five other National Guards-men were on duty in Orangeburg that night. As Maceo Nance, president of the college, later observed, "With the police power on hand, they could have arrested the entire college community if they had wanted to."

The shootings climaxed four days of increasingly unruly protests over students being denied access to a local all-white bowling alley. On the second night of protests, a number of students, including several coeds, had been clubbed when they attempted to force their way into the bowling alley. Eight students and a police officer had been briefly hospitalized after that encounter.

Dozier Mobley, an AP photographer who witnessed the shootings, told me that on the night of the shootings he didn't hear any shots from the campus before the troopers opened fire. But he said that just before a line of approximately ten state troopers opened fire, one trooper may have touched off the barrage when, upon seeing another officer felled by a missile hurled by a student, yelled, "Get down, they're shooting at us."

Mobley said, "The police panicked. I was surprised and disappointed. They lost their composure. They were running around and shouting and hollering. It was bad."

I asked Henry Lake, an attorney and Governor McNair's official representative on the scene, about Mobley's comment that the officers panicked and were running around and shouting. "He doesn't understand policemen," Lake said. "They weren't doing any such damn thing. They ran and got under cover, that's the first thing an officer is supposed to do. They had to do that to protect their lives, there was no other way out."

As for evidence that students were shot in their backs, Lake said, "Some of the students were trying to get the hell out of there, they wished to hell they had not been there, and some could have been hit when they turned their backs to run."

McNair, Lake, and other officials blamed the entire episode on "outside agitators," and repeatedly fingered Cleveland Sellers, a twenty-three-year-old organizer for the Student Nonviolent Coordinating Committee and the only person arrested the night of the shootings. Sellers, who grew up in Denmark, eighteen miles from Orangeburg, was charged with inciting to riot, arson, breaking and entering, larceny, and assault and battery. Sellers, who earlier had told a reporter that if trouble broke out he no doubt would be the "scapegoat," was hustled off to the state penitentiary.

Sellers, who was not a South Carolina State student, had helped organize the college's Black Awareness Coordinating Committee. Lake said authorities had been unable to "pinpoint" any offenses by the committee—except for Sellers's role. "He's the main man," Lake told me. "He's the biggest nigger in the crowd."

People who knew Sellers well found the charges against him unbelievable. My friend Chuck Morgan, by then the southern director of the

ACLU, told me he found Sellers to be "a gentlemanly person who is easy to deal with."

"I've seen him at places as varied as my office, a lecture platform at an Ohio college, and the coaches' All-American football game in Atlanta," Morgan said. "He is a man of varied interests, and it is inconceivable to me that he would have initiated action which would have been in any way responsible for the tragedy Thursday night. His sole responsibility, it would seem to me, rests in the fact that he has told Negroes for a number of years that they are entitled to the rights of other American citizens, and, since the passage of the 1964 Civil Rights Act, to the pursuit of happiness. This, it seems to me, includes the use of public accommodations such as the bowling alley in a little southern town where the major industry is the education of Negro students."

Along with Jack Bass, a dogged reporter for the *Charlotte Observer* at the time who also covered the shootings, I began digging further into the episodes, and eventually the two of us wrote a book, *The Orangeburg Massacre*. Among other things, we exposed the fact that three FBI agents witnessed the shootings, but had denied to Justice Department civil rights lawyers that they had been witnesses. They also filed an investigative report two months after the shootings that failed to mention they were witnesses and that tended to exonerate the troopers. We contacted the FBI agents and questioned them about that but they refused to comment, one of them declaring, "I don't want to get into a pissing contest with civil rights attorneys."

Ramsey Clark, the attorney general at the time, told me that, during the Orangeburg investigation, civil rights attorneys "had quite a bit of trouble with a number of FBI agents as to what they said at different times, and we had trouble getting all the interviews we wanted. We also had a terribly difficult time finding out where the FBI people were on the night of February 8—where they were, what they were doing, whether they were witnesses."

In covering civil rights, I found that strained relations between the FBI and the civil rights attorneys was nothing new, because agents often considered civil rights enforcement a thankless or even odious task, especially when it involved accusations against police officials with whom they routinely worked and often socialized. In addition, many agents were southerners themselves who, not surprisingly, harbored the usual prejudices against blacks.

Dr. Martin Luther King Jr., in one of his last communications with federal officials before his assassination in Memphis on April 4, wired Clark that the shootings "must not go unpunished." King demanded that the government "act now to bring to justice the perpetrators of the largest armed assault undertaken under color of law in recent southern history."

Clark himself had found the police action indefensible and didn't let the FBI's lack of interest in pursuing the case deter him. He ordered a thorough investigation headed by Stephen Pollak, head of the Justice Department's Civil Rights Division. And by September, about seven months after the shootings, Pollak was ready to seek an indictment against nine state troopers under a law making it a federal offense for anyone, acting under color of law, to subject any person to deprivation of federally protected rights. But the burden of presenting the case to a federal grand jury fell to Chad Quaintance, a young civil rights attorney, because Klyde Robinson, the local U. S. attorney, refused to participate in the case.

The grand jury, made up of twenty-three whites and two blacks, refused to return an indictment. But Pollak, after reading a transcript of the grand jury testimony, concluded that evidence was sufficient to bring the troopers to trial under a criminal information filed by the Justice Department. He knew the chances of getting a conviction would be slim but thought that trial in open court—regardless of the verdict—would have a deterrent effect on police misconduct. The trial was held, but it took the jury of ten whites and two blacks less than two hours to return not guilty verdicts.

More than two and a half years after the shootings, the state of South Carolina, which never investigated the shootings nor even held an inquest into the three deaths, did bring Cleveland Sellers to trial. They tried him on three charges of riot after dropping four other charges they had brought against him. Despite a paucity of evidence, Sellers was found guilty by a jury of nine whites and three blacks and was sentenced to a year in prison.

When *The Orangeburg Massacre* was published in 1970, J. Edgar Hoover wrote a letter to Jack Bass declaring that the book contained "a number of irresponsible allegations." Since Hoover already had ordered FBI agents to have nothing to do with me as a result of the disclosures I made about another case—the FBI's role in planning the assassination of a Klansman in Meridian, Mississippi—he didn't correspond with me or even send me a copy of his letter to Bass. But Hoover, who did not brook the slightest criticism, still had me in his sights.

Insofar as the Orangeburg case was concerned, Hoover denied, among other things, that FBI agents were on the scene at the time of the shootings, and he concluded by declaring that "the book is so biased in its attempts to smear the FBI that it raises serious questions as to the competence and objectivity of the authors."

In a letter to Hoover, Bass cited irrefutable evidence that three FBI agents were on the scene and he refuted other accusations point by point. "I find no substantive error in the book as it pertains to the FBI or any other group or individual," Bass wrote. "The facts in this episode are unkind to many."

Hoover fired back a brief reply declaring Bass's statement about "no substantive error" would not stand up "under analysis." But he offered no further substantiation and concluded not by citing any alleged mistakes but by declaring, that "in regard to your book as a whole it reminds me of the 'scissors and paste' method of writing and arguing."

In a newspaper interview just before leaving office in 1971, Governor McNair characterized the Orangeburg book as "more fiction than . . . fact, " but offered no specifics. And in his final address to the state legislature he conceded that what happened at Orangeburg was "a scar on our state's conscience."

Many years later another governor would officially apologize for the armed assault on students on their own campus. In a thirty-third anniversary ceremony held February 8, 2000, on the South Carolina State campus, Governor Jim Hodges said, "We deeply regret what happened here on the night of February 8, 1968. The Orangeburg Massacre was a great tragedy for our state. Even today, the state of South Carolina bows its head, bends its knee and begins the search for reconciliation."

Cleveland Sellers, who served seven months in prison after he was convicted of "riot," went on to earn a master's degree in education at Harvard, became a faculty member at the University of South Carolina, and was recently named president of Voorhees College. He characterized himself as a political prisoner who had committed no crime and predicted his conviction would eventually be overturned.

More than twenty years later, in July 1993, with the valuable assistance of Jack Bass, who wrote a strong letter recommending Sellers be pardoned, the seven-member state probation, pardon and parole board unanimously voted to grant him a pardon.

Through perseverance and a commitment to not let the state forget about what happened at the college campus, Bass, by now Professor

Emeritus at the College of Charleston, has kept *The Orangeburg Massacre* updated in subsequent editions, and it continues to be published by Mercer University Press. The book is still widely read and used as part of courses in high schools and colleges in South Carolina.

Chapter 21

TRAVELS WITH GEORGE

GEORGE CORLEY WALLACE, the fiery Alabama governor remembered for boasting he would defend "segregation today, segregation tomorrow, and segregation forever," harangued a lot of reporters over his long political career. But knowing that I was a native of Alabama and that I didn't mind pressing him with thorny questions at press conferences, he relished singling me out at his political rallies for his own special brand of ridicule.

As my friend Ray Jenkins, an *Alabama Journal* editor at the time who covered Wallace for years, once wrote of our relationship, "A few newsmen have so incurred the Governor's wrath that he holds a permanent grudge. Nelson has written so sharply about Wallace, has pressed uncomfortable questions so relentlessly at press conferences, that Wallace is given to making savage jabs at him in public as well as private."

Ours was a complicated relationship. Wallace angrily resented what I wrote, but I think somewhere down deep he had a sneaking fondness for his fellow Alabamian. And he was always accessible to me. When I would show up at his office in the state capitol to interview him, he would say, "Come on in. I know you're goin' to distort what I have to say, but come on in anyway. You fellas always puttin' things in the paper I don't say." Still, he didn't hesitate to use me as a foil. At political rallies he would draw raucous laughter and sometimes muttered threats by pointing me out and shouting in his thick drawl, "Thay he is, out there from the *Los A-n-g-e-l-e-e-s Times*. Out there where they give blood to the Veet Cong, fly the Veet Cong flag! Look at him, ah made 'im get 'is hair cut!"

After about the fifth time he repeated that I approached him after the rally and said, "Governor, how come you always tell folks you made me get a haircut? As long as you've known me I've had a flat-top haircut."

Wallace, always quick with a snappy retort, narrowed his eyes and said, "Well, let's put it this way, about half what you write about me is so and about half what I say about you is so."

I always quoted Wallace in the vernacular, using apostrophes when he would drop the "g" from words like "getting" and "putting." And I knew Wallace read my stories about his campaigning because E. C. Dothard, one of his beefy bodyguards, came up to me one day and said, "The guvner sho' is mad at you."

"What have I done now, why's he so mad?" I asked. The bodyguard looked at me, smiled wryly, draped a muscular arm over my shoulders, and said, "He's getting' goddamn sick and tired of you always usin' them 'postrophes when you quote him."

At another rally Wallace teed off on me while some of his rowdier supporters began yelling threats like, "They ought to kill the little son of a bitch." Floyd Jemison, another of his burly bodyguards, sidled up to me, winked, and whispered, "The guv'nor said not to worry, I'm to look out for you if the crowd gets too worked up." I didn't find it very reassuring.

The state troopers who protected Wallace revered him and shared his view of the press. Once when several of us reporters were following Wallace into a roadside café, I was introduced as a *Los Angeles Times* reporter to a trooper newly assigned to protect Wallace. The trooper eyed me with loathing and, completely out of the blue, exclaimed: "Well, I can tell you one goddamn thing, there ain't but three people can walk on water— Jesus Christ, [Alabama football coach] Bear Bryant, and George Wallace. And don't you forget it."

For all of Wallace's crowd-pleasing barbs, he spoke so angrily at times that he inflamed the emotions of supporters and hecklers alike. Along with other veteran political reporters I sometimes described audience reaction as "scary" and "chilling." When Wallace first ran for president as the candidate of the American Independent Party in 1968, an atmosphere of hate permeated almost every political rally. His followers cheered lustily when he threatened to "run over" protesters or to appoint an attorney general who would "drag 'em by their long hair and put 'em under the jail."

He sneered at "pseudointellectuals who can tell us how to get out of Vietnam but can't park their bicycles straight" and he ridiculed "pointy-headed reporters who don't tell folks about what big crowds I get."

Wallace's fiery rhetoric frequently touched off fights between protesters and supporters, and occasionally police would move in and assault disorderly demonstrators. Although he charged that news reports exaggerated violence at his rallies, he clearly relished the trouble and even told me, "It gets me votes."

At the smallest sign of a scuffle among protesters and supporters at his rallies, he would shout, "Let the police handle it. Those are some of the people the country is sick and tired of." It made no difference that the trouble had been started by his supporters. He would blame the "an-ar-chists" and the crowd would cheer lustily. "If when ah'm president, any an-ar-chists lie down in front of my automobile," he'd say, "it'll be the last time they lie down in front of anything."

On October 3, 1968, during Wallace's campaign for president, he introduced retired Air Force General Curtis E. LeMay of World War II fame as his vice presidential running mate at a press conference in Pittsburgh, Pennsylvania. LeMay, a truculent anti-Communist hard-liner, had directed the Strategic Air Command into a force capable of waging a nuclear war against the Soviet Union if that became necessary. In 1965 LeMay's saber rattling upset many Americans when he declared that his solution to ending the war against the North Vietnamese was to "tell them frankly that they've got to draw in their horns and stop their aggression or we're going to bomb them back into the Stone Age."

So it should have come as no surprise to Wallace when the press conference quickly turned into a fiasco for his candidacy after I asked LeMay what policy he would follow about deciding whether to use nuclear weapons.

While Wallace grimaced, LeMay plunged headlong into the subject. "We seem to have a phobia about nuclear weapons," LeMay said in a long, tortuous reply that left no doubt he favored using nuclear weapons under certain circumstances. "I think that most military men think nuclear weapons are just another weapon in the arsenal and the smart thing to do is when you're in a war—hopefully you prevent it and stay out of it if you can—but when you get in it, get in it with both feet and get it over with soon as you can. Use the force that's necessary, maybe use a little bit more to make sure that it's enough to stop the fighting as soon as possible."

LeMay was on a roll and Wallace nervously paced off to the side, clasping his hands and grimacing as the general continued, declaring that while nuclear war would be horrible, any war is horrible. "It doesn't make much difference to me that if I have to go to war and get killed in the jungle of Vietnam with a rusty knife or get killed with a nuclear weapon. Matter of fact, I'd lean toward the nuclear weapon."

The more LeMay talked, the deeper the hole he dug. "So I don't believe the world will end if we explode a nuclear weapon," he said. "But on the other hand I don't want to explode one unless we have to. And as a matter of fact I don't want to stick a rusty knife into anybody's belly either. I think you have to be pretty practical about these things."

As the press conference drew to a close and LeMay started to leave, I shouted at Wallace and asked him whether he agreed with what LeMay had said about using nuclear weapons. LeMay suddenly whirled around and said, "I didn't get the question." Wallace, his lips pursed, his face flushed, and his jaw jutted, leaned over to the general and said, "They said you agreed to use nuclear weapons. You didn't say it!"

LeMay frowned and his eyes widened as he turned quickly to the microphone and declared, "I gave you a discussion on the phobia we have in this country about the use of nuclear weapons! I prefer not to use them! I prefer not to use any weapon at all! I don't think it's necessary at this stage of the game to use them!"

"If you find it necessary to end the war would you use them?" I asked.

LeMay didn't hesitate. "If I find it necessary I would use anything we could dream up, including nuclear weapons—if it was necessary. I don't think it's necessary at this stage of the game."

As Wallace hurried over and started leading LeMay from the lectern, I quickly shouted, "Governor Wallace, do you agree with him?"

Wallace, his face contorted in anger, hurried back to the microphone and declared, "What you're doing, Mr. Nelson—is typical of the *Los Angeles Times*—is you're trying to say that if the time ever came that it was necessary to use any sort of weapon in the vital interests of the country, you wouldn't use 'em. All General LeMay has said—and I know you fellows better than he does because I've had to deal with you—he said that if the security of the country depended upon the use of any weapon in the future, he would use it. But he prefers not to use any weapon. He prefers to negotiate."

But LeMay jumped in again with another damaging remark. "Let's get this thing straight. I know that I'm going to come out with a lot of misquotes in this campaign. I have in the past. And I'll be damned lucky if I don't appear as a drooling idiot whose only solution to any problem is to drop atomic bombs all over the world. I assure you I'm not . . . My desire is to not use any weapons. But once the time comes to fight, I would use any weapons in the arsenal ready as necessary . . ."

Wallace finally managed to persuade LeMay to leave the podium. And then to get the general out of the news, he dispatched him on a fact-finding tour of Vietnam before beginning a ten-day barnstorming tour of his own across the country to San Francisco.

At the time of the press conference, the Harris poll had 21 percent of the American people favoring Wallace for president. By the time he arrived in San Francisco a week later his poll number had dropped to 13 percent and his mood was souring. On his trip west my colleague Nicholas Chriss covered Wallace's campaign for the *Los Angeles Times* and noted that the size of his rallies had fallen off considerably in the wake of the disastrous Pittsburgh press conference.

Shortly afterwards, I was back on the campaign trail with Wallace at San Francisco's Cow Palace where police were kept busy protecting several hundred protesters from more than ten thousand boisterous Wallace supporters. "Kill the hippies, kill the hippies," some of the supporters shouted. But overall Wallace got a rousing reception from supporters who drowned out the protesters, and I wrote that the rally was a high point in what otherwise had been "a rather disappointing, week-long western tour" for the governor.

The next day as we were flying out of California on Wallace's campaign plane, he came stomping down the aisle to the press section waving a copy of the morning's *Los Angeles Times*. He stopped beside me, thrust the paper under my face, and said, "I see where you say we didn't get no good crowds 'til we got to San Francisco. Shee-it, you weren't even with us 'til we got to San Francisco."

"Well, governor," I said, "Nick Chriss was with you and he said you didn't get any good crowds 'til you got to San Francisco."

"Shee-it," he drawled. "I know you and the *Los Angeles Times*. You don't want to see me get no good crowds." With that he whirled around and stomped back up to the front of the plane.

Despite the LeMay fiasco and Wallace's drop in opinion polls, in 1968 he still made one of the strongest showings ever for a third-party candidate in a presidential election. While former Republican Vice President Richard Nixon scored a close victory over Democratic Senator Hubert Humphrey, Wallace won almost ten million votes and carried five southern states.

Four years later, on May 15, 1972, Humphrey, as the Democratic nominee, and Wallace, as an independent, were again running for president against Nixon. I was covering Humphrey when it was announced on the senator's campaign plane that Wallace had been shot while campaigning in Laurel, Maryland. Michelle Clark, a pretty young black correspondent for CBS who later died in a plane accident, turned to me and exclaimed, "Oh God, don't let the shooter be black!"

The shooter turned out to be an apparently deranged twenty-one-year-old white, Arthur Bremer, who fired five bullets into Wallace as the governor shook hands with some of the more than one thousand people who had gathered to hear him at a shopping center. Wallace survived, but he was paralyzed and confined to a wheelchair for the rest of his life. Some of the bullets went through Wallace and struck two male guards as well as a female spectator, but they all recovered. Bremer was convicted of assault with intent to kill and sentenced to fifty-three years.

Wallace was hospitalized and unable to campaign for the next six presidential primaries of 1972. He returned to the campaign trail and eventually finished third behind Senator George McGovern, the nominee, and former Vice President Hubert Humphrey.

Wallace's near-death experience had a profound impact on him, transforming his views on race. He became much more subdued, and the fiery rhetoric disappeared. He began to reach out to blacks and apologize for his past positions on race. In 1974 he was strongly supported by blacks when he was reelected as governor. In 1976 he ran for the presidency on the Democratic ticket, but finished dismally behind Jimmy Carter who went on to win.

When Wallace's term as governor ended in 1979 he did not seek reelection, but began a series of lectures at universities and other venues where he abjectly apologized for his segregationist past. Speaking at the Dexter Avenue Baptist Church in Montgomery where Dr. Martin Luther King Jr. had been pastor, Wallace said his own crippling injuries and close call with death had made him more aware of others' problems and had led to a change of heart.

Speaking from his wheelchair, he told the congregation, "I have learned what suffering means in a way that was impossible before. I think I can understand something of the pain that black people have come to endure. I know I contributed to that pain, and I can only ask for your forgiveness." The congregation applauded and afterwards members crowded around and shook his hand.

Wallace ran for governor one more time, in 1982, and he went on Alabama public television and addressed the Southern Christian Leadership

Conference that had been headed by Dr. King to once again apologize for his past support of segregation. He carried about a third of the black vote in winning the Democratic nomination over Lieutenant Governor George McMillan and then carried the vast majority of the black vote in soundly defeating the Republican nominee, Montgomery Mayor Emory Folmer.

In 1989, in an exchange of correspondence I had with Wallace, he proudly wrote about his support among blacks and the large number of blacks he had appointed to important state positions. We corresponded after I had been selected, as a native Alabamian, for an annual Living for America award by the Alabama State Bureau of Travel and Tourism, the city of Selma, and Selma–Dallas County Chamber of Commerce, the same award Wallace had received several years earlier.

After announcement of the award, Wallace wrote a letter congratulating me and explaining why he couldn't travel to Selma for the award ceremony.

> Dr. Jack:
>
> I am certainly sorry that I cannot be with you in Selma on August 17. However, I would like to congratulate you . . .
>
> I always enjoyed my visits with you, and I always remember the press conference you attended where General LeMay answered questions.
>
> I also enjoyed your visiting us in Alabama, and I hope some day I may see you again. However, as I explained in the letter to those who invited me, I am physically unable to get into an automobile and can ride a very little distance in a van because it is so painful to me.
>
> Again, congratulations and I hope our paths will cross some day.
>
> With kind personal regards, I am
> Sincerely yours,
> George C. Wallace

After the award ceremony, I wrote Wallace a letter in reply:

> Dear Gov. Wallace:
>
> I'm sorry I didn't get to see you when I was in Selma, but I really appreciated the nice letter you sent.
>
> I enjoyed our visits in the past, too, even when you'd greet me and say—half-joking, I hope—"Come on in, I know you're gonna distort it."

The Pittsburgh press conference where you announced Gen. Curtis LeMay as your running mate is indelibly imprinted in my mind, too. I vividly recall how you tried to get the general to stop answering questions and said something like, "I know how to handle you folks from the *Los Angeles Times*, but the general doesn't know." Anyway, you had a hard time dragging him away because he insisted on answering questions.

I was terribly sorry to hear that you are unable to get into an automobile and can ride only a short distance in a van because it is so painful to you. . . .

Of all the public figures I've covered in more than 40 years as a reporter you rank right at the top as one of the most interesting and politically astute. I wrote a story today about the changes in Selma and quoted a black attorney, J. L. Chestnut Jr., as saying you were one of the most gifted politicians he had ever met.

Thanks again for the nice letter you wrote and the congratulations you extended. I, too, hope our paths will cross again. And I hope your life here on out is a little easier and free of pain.

Sincerely yours,
Jack Nelson

In reply, Wallace wrote about how proud he was of the support he had received from black voters and how, as governor, he had produced programs that benefited blacks:

Dear Jack:

I appreciated your long letter after your visit to Selma. I only wish that I could have been there to see you again.

For your information, in 1974 I received 95% of the black vote in Alabama for Governor. Some of the predominately black counties—75 to 80%—vied with each other to see who would give me the largest vote. Sumter County, which has all black officials and is 75 to 80% black, gave me 98.2% of the vote. Greene County, which has all black officials and is 80% black, gave me 95% of the vote. The two all white counties (Winston and DeKalb) gave me 86.5% of the vote.

I appointed more black judges, more black cabinet members, more black board of trustees members, more blacks on the Prison Board, Ethics Board, Pardon and Parole Board, Personnel Board, etc. than any other governor in Alabama's history. I also received an honorary doctorate degree from Tuskegee University on Founder's Day in 1986 honoring Booker T. Washington and George Washington Carver. This is one of the most thrilling awards I have received during my career. I received 95% of the black vote in the 1982 election. My last press secretary was a black named Frank Mastin, who is a former major in the United States Army, having fought in Vietnam. He was one of the best press secretaries I ever had.

The University of Alabama has a scientific poll called the Capstone Poll. As I was going out of office in 1986, which is when you are at your lowest ebb, the question was asked by them, and the results appeared on the front page of the *Birmingham News*, "Do you believe that George Wallace was the best governor Alabama ever had?" Fifty-two percent said yes and 42% said no. They broke it down into categories. Whites: 50/50%. Blacks: 74% yes, 26% no. So, you see, the black people of Alabama know that I did more for them in the matter of technical schools and junior college. I gave their children a chance to go off to one of these schools which are within bus distance, and we drove them in by bus each day as they do now. . . .

Again, let me say that it is always good to have been with you, and I hope our paths will cross again. I would, of course, have been with you in Selma except that I cannot ride in an automobile anymore, as you know.

Again, thank you for your long letter. I hope to see you again one of these days.

With kind regards to you and our mutual friends in the press, I am

Sincerely yours,
George C. Wallace

Wallace died on September 13, 1998, and shortly thereafter John Lewis, the civil rights leader who by then was a well-established Georgia congressman, told the *New York Times*, "With all his failings, Mr. Wallace deserves recognition for seeking redemption for his mistakes, for his willingness to change and to set things straight with those he harmed and with his God."

I shared John Lewis's views about Wallace and his redemption and always regretted I never got back to Montgomery to see him after our exchange of correspondence. He was, without question, one of the most fascinating as well as one of the most demagogic politicians I covered in all my years as a reporter.

Chapter 22

MARTIN LUTHER KING JR.: FROM GEE'S BEND TO MEMPHIS

I OFTEN THINK HOW LUCKY I was to report on Martin Luther King Jr. at a time when his credo of nonviolence was still a powerful, inspirational force. I had been covering him for only two weeks when he left Selma briefly to carry his voting rights drive to nearby Gee's Bend, a tiny all-black community in the backwoods of Alabama. The contrast between the adulation he received there and what happened at the end of my coverage of his demonstrations in Memphis three years later could not have been starker.

We journalists followed King nearly everywhere he went in the South. It was an all-consuming, exhilarating assignment, and I felt proud to be a member of his admiring, largely white press corps. It was not our admiration that made him such hot copy. He was uncommonly adept at making news. Plus, for the white news media, he often served as a convenient stand-in for the whole civil rights movement, though this was a gross oversimplification. The truth is, it was a lot harder for us to cover other aspects of the movement, such as the fieldwork conducted by the Student Nonviolent Coordinating Committee, popularly known as Snick. SNCC sent hundreds of young field workers to live in some of the most dangerous places in the South, trying to organize poor, illiterate blacks, but it was King and his marches that commanded our attention.

I covered King as often as I could, though I frequently had to break away for other stories. The *New York Times*, which usually fielded more than one person in the South, had a reporter assigned to King virtually at all times—a precaution in case he was assassinated. The prospect of violence, we knew, was never absent from the potent mix of crowds, TV cameras, and naked hatred that swirled around him.

From the beginning of his quest for civil rights, King realized that press coverage was essential for the movement to succeed. And, for the most part, he carried on a friendly but fairly formal and businesslike relationship with reporters. None of my colleagues that I can recall could ever buddy up to him. Although the press and the movement organizers were all close to the same age in the mid-1960s when I began covering him—most of us were in our thirties and he was in his midthirties—he always addressed us formally, using the honorific "Mister." We called him "Dr. King." He addressed the rare female reporter covering civil rights in those days as "Miss."

"Mr. Nelson, you goin' with us to Gee's Bend tomorrow?" he asked me one day in Selma, apparently concerned that some of the national press that had been covering him in Selma might not be interested in following him to such a small community, where he planned to press his drive to increase voter registration.

"Dr. King, I wouldn't miss it," I assured him, although at the time I didn't quite understand why he would leave Selma to attend a rally in such a relatively unknown, out-of-the-way community. Once we arrived at Gee's Bend I understood why he would stage a rally there. It provided a dramatic scene made to order for the kind of news coverage—especially by television and large newspapers—that King courted, knowing it helped build national sentiment in support of the civil rights movement.

Outside the dilapidated frame church where King spoke it was bitterly cold. And inside the only heat came from a pot-bellied stove. Except for television klieg lights, the only light was provided by a naked lightbulb hanging from a single wire at the front of the church.

Along with dozens of other reporters, I sat transfixed as King looked over an audience of some three hundred black faces, most if not all of them direct descendants of slaves. He talked of how the Negro, after centuries of suppression under slavery and then segregation, "had come to feel that he doesn't count, that he was nobody."

"I come over here in Gee's Bend to tell you, you are somebody," he thundered in those majestic cadences of the black Baptist preacher that he was. "Every man from a bass black to a treble white is significant on God's keyboard. You may not know the difference between 'you does' and 'you don't,' but you are as good as the best white person in Wilcox County!"

It may have been the first time anyone had told them they were "somebody," and it certainly was the first time anyone had told them they were as good as any white person in the county.

As King spoke, tears streamed down his face. Old women, sitting in straight-back chairs in front of the church, many of them bundled in sweaters and wearing head scarves with knots tied in the front, applauded wildly and called out again and again, "It's true, it's true." By the time he finished there was hardly a dry eye in the house. Even reporters, including myself, teared up.

King was speaking in one of the most deprived areas of the Black Belt—an all-Negro community of 116 families and a population of 700. Located about forty miles southwest of Selma, Gee's Bend is in Wilcox County, where Negroes then comprised 75 percent of the population but had no registered voters.

Located in a bend of the Alabama River, Gee's Bend was a place where life stood still. To get there, we had to travel along six miles of treacherous, muddy road at a time when no white community in Alabama was without access by paved roads. King was used to the mud. Ever since he had launched the Black Belt voter registration campaign in October 1963, he had frequently stayed at the Torch Motel in Selma, a four-unit brick lodging for Negroes which, when it rained, was surrounded by mud. There were no paved streets anywhere in the immediate vicinity.

In his speech to the Benders, as they were known, King described the community's dilapidated high school as a "disgrace" and told blacks that they could get better roads and schools once they obtained political power through getting the right to vote. At that time in Alabama's Black Belt, a region actually stretching across the Deep South and so called because of both its rich black soil and heavy black population, there were nineteen counties. Of Negroes over twenty-five years of age in those counties, 67 percent had less than a sixth-grade education. By contrast, among the white population, 82 percent had better than a sixth-grade education.

King unquestionably knew that the high illiteracy rate in Gee's Bend would preclude registration of most of its residents. But he had another audience in mind. The rally there was aimed more at building nationwide support for a new voting rights law than it was to get the local Negroes registered. At that moment, events were on his side. The brutality of the attack on peaceful demonstrators in Selma early in March and the murders that were connected with it had accelerated the movement for passage of the voting rights bill. Lyndon Johnson signed it into law on August 6, 1965, with King, Roy Wilkins, John Lewis, and other civil rights leaders looking on.

We didn't know it at the time, of course, but the passage of the act was probably the high-water mark of the civil rights movement as well as for Dr. King's doctrine of nonviolence. Just days after the passage of the voting rights bill, the Watts district of Los Angeles erupted in flames. When the riot was over six days later, thirty-four people were dead, more than a thousand injured, and some three thousand arrested. The following year rioting broke out in Chicago, Cleveland, San Francisco, and Atlanta—the city too busy to hate—as well as in numerous smaller cities.

Chicago, in particular, represented a fiasco for Dr. King. He had gone there against the advice of his advisers to try to prove that nonviolence could work in the North. After six months in which little was accomplished in the way of better housing or more jobs for blacks, he led a march into an all-white neighborhood on August 5, 1966, to demand an open housing law and the end of redlining. There, he and about eight hundred demonstrators were met by a thousand screaming, jeering whites, many hurling rocks and bottles. One rock struck Dr. King, knocking him to the pavement. He looked shaken as aides surrounded him and helped him to his feet. "I have seen many demonstrations in the South but I have never seen anything so hostile and so hateful as I've seen here today," he stated.

A few months later, he was forced to admit defeat after an agreement with city agencies and banks to build and finance more public housing produced no results. "It appears that for all intents and purposes, the public agencies have [reneged] on the agreement and have, in fact, given credence to those who proclaim the housing agreement a sham and a batch of false promises."

At the same time, King was up against the growing schisms within the movement, coupled with direct challenges to his leadership. Younger movement blacks, in particular members of SNCC, had grown restive with his gradualism and tendency to compromise, his willingness to sit down and negotiate with white officialdom. Behind his back, they called him "De Lawd."

Stokely Carmichael, a firebrand who was also a highly effective organizer, posed the most direct threat to King's leadership. I was present at a meeting in Atlanta on May 17, 1966, when it was announced that Carmichael was replacing John Lewis, a moderate and close associate of Dr. King, as chairman of SNCC. If there was anyone I admired as much as Dr. King, it was John Lewis. A man with a mystical and religious bent, he used to say that lightning and snakes—those two great southern bugaboos—were the only things he was afraid of. We journalists didn't think John Lewis was afraid of anything. During the sixties he was arrested forty times and beaten so often he lost count. But he just bowed his head and came back for more. On Bloody Sunday, he suffered a fractured skull as he led the march across the Edmund Pettus Bridge.

Lewis was obviously bitter over the demotion. I felt for him when he tried to answer reporters' questions but was cut off by several SNCC members, who curtly informed us that a newly formed central committee would release all information. In fact the atmosphere in the room was distinctly surly to us white newsmen, and Lewis confirmed that the organization was moving in an all-Negro direction, though he said he did not agree with the policy. After the meeting broke up, I went up to Stokely and said, "You can't mean that you're not going to cooperate with white reporters any more?," pointing out that most of us were in sympathy with efforts to achieve justice for blacks. Carmichael retorted, "Oh no?" He said, "Just watch us."

Only days later, in a famous speech at a rally in Greenwood, Mississippi, Carmichael launched his call for "Black Power!" This was a new Stokely. The old Stokely was an amiable civil rights worker who had good relationships with reporters covering the South. Two of his close friends were white civil rights volunteers—Father Richard Morrisroe, a Catholic priest, and Jonathan Daniels, an Episcopal ministerial student. But a white deputy sheriff in Lowndes County killed Daniels with a shotgun blast at close range and nearly killed Father Morrisroe with a blast in the back as he turned to run. An all-white jury—the only kind they had in Lowndes County—acquitted the man charged with the killing.

Friends of Carmichael said the shootings and the trial had a traumatic effect on him. He became distrustful of practically all whites. I could see the changes in him, watching as he turned bitter and cynical, cursing his country and saying that democracy was a failure.

Although fissures in the movement had been growing for a while, the tensions between the Old Guard and the Young Turks were now out in the open, with Dr. King's call for "Freedom Now!" increasingly replaced by the black power slogan. In an interview I had with King ten days after Carmichael's speech, he was openly critical of the SNCC leader and his call for black power. He said it "confused a lot of our white friends" and had engendered "a misguided hatred of white people among some Negroes." Black power as such was all right, he said, but the way the slogan was used by SNCC gave the impression that blacks were seeking supremacy. "All groups have to have power to exist in the mainstream of American life, and I have been preaching 'black power' for years. But I believe in a shared power, blacks and whites working together. It would give us all—the whites as well—more power."

The SNCC meeting in Atlanta was the first time I recall feeling unwelcome at a black gathering in the South. We reporters were used to being looked on as the good guys. In the North, however, covering the race story was already becoming dangerous. *Newsweek's* Carl Fleming, a superb reporter who had been transferred from the Atlanta bureau to Los Angeles, got a fractured skull and had both jaws broken while covering the 1965 riot in Watts. It would soon become dangerous in the South as well. A year later, on September 6, 1966, when a riot broke out in the impoverished Summerville neighborhood of Atlanta, I found myself surrounded by an angry crowd of African Americans who looked intent on beating me up. I got away by running up side streets back to the office, but it was a close call. Roy Reed was lucky that day too. He was standing on a corner talking to Andy Young, one of Dr. King's top lieutenants, when they saw a noisy mob approaching. Young turned to a young woman with him and said, "Can you drive a car?" She said yes. He said, "Get into that car and put Mr. Reed in there and get him out of here in a hurry." She did.

It is ironic, but as the civil rights drive continued to falter and more cities erupted in flames, King's international reputation was at its zenith. His stature was deserved in my view. After all, he had become a heroic and historic figure for spearheading a peaceful movement that led to dramatic changes: congressional passage of the 1964 public accommodations law and the 1965 voting rights law. And he had been awarded the highly coveted Nobel Peace Prize. But controversy continued to swirl around him as he shifted his focus from civil rights to economic justice and opposition to the war in Vietnam.

In an effort to regain the initiative in 1968, King announced a massive Poor People's Campaign to take place in Washington to press for jobs and housing. Planning was under way for the campaign that March when King decided he needed to go to Memphis. His purpose was to try to force the city administration to settle a lengthy strike by the city's nearly all-black garbage workers. So he and Reverend James Lawson, the head of Memphis's Community on the Move for Equality, began leading a protest march they hoped would press the city to come to terms with the strikers.

Those hopes were dashed when the demonstration turned violent. Hundreds of young toughs broke from the several thousand demonstrators and began smashing windows and looting stores. King's aides, alarmed by the violence, summoned police who escorted him and Lawson to safety. And I, along with scores of other reporters covering the chaos, quickly melted in with the peaceful demonstrators to escape the chaos and violence. By the time Memphis police and Tennessee National Guardsmen restored order, four blacks had been shot, one of them fatally; about three hundred others had been injured. Rioters had started more than a hundred fires.

Even before the Memphis rioting, which marked the first time a King-led demonstration had spawned widespread violence by the participants, some civil rights leaders had told me they were concerned that the Poor People's Campaign was fraught with potential danger. A Memphis civil rights leader told me, "Martin can't make it anymore because the mood of the country is different. He couldn't make it in Chicago. He almost abandoned the South and got lost in the peace movement. He needed a victory in Memphis. I've heard Martin talk of turning dark midnights into glittering days of sunshine, but he can't do it this time. Washington will be his Waterloo." But it turned out that Memphis would be his Waterloo.

After the demonstration ended in violence, King sounded mortified as he confessed to reporters that he had failed to take into account the violent mood of young militants and said, "Our intelligence was totally nil." But I wrote that he should have had ample reason to have known about the potential for violence because Lawson had told me he had warned King and his aides about the presence of militants bent on a rampage. King also insisted the Poor People's Campaign he planned to begin in Washington on April 23 would be peaceful. However, other civil rights leaders, including Bayard Rustin, who had coordinated the massive 1963 Washington demonstration where King made his famous "I have a dream" speech, told me they opposed the demonstrations, partly out of fear of violence and partly because of the realization that demonstrations could no longer pressure Congress into enacting economic and social reforms King was demanding.

Early in April, King headed back to Memphis to live up to a promise to lead another march that he guaranteed would be peaceful. I was there the night before the rally, on April 3, 1968, in the spacious Mason Temple, when his rhetoric soared to new heights. He brought a huge crowd of demonstrators to their feet, applauding and cheering as he talked darkly and expansively about all the death threats and close brushes with death he had experienced leading up to his Memphis rallies.

Reporters, covering his speech from the balcony and writing furiously on their notepads and fiddling with their tape recorders, were glued to King's every word. We exchanged glances that meant, "Can you believe he's talking like this?"

Finally King, sweating profusely, his eyes glistening, concluded with a soaring peroration in slow cadences that reporters later agreed sounded like a premonition:

> Well, I don't know what will happen now. We've got some difficult days ahead. It doesn't matter what happens to me now. Because I've been to the mountaintop. And I don't mind. Like anybody, I would like to live a long life. Longevity has its place. But I'm not concerned about that now. I just want to do God's will. And he's allowed me to go up to the mountain. And I've looked over. And I've seen the promised land! I may not get there with you. But I want you to know tonight that we, as a people, will get to the promised land! And I'm happy tonight. I'm not worried about anything. I'm not fearing any man! Mine eyes have seen the glory of the coming of the Lord! His truth is marching on!

King sat down, seemingly exhausted, and wiped his face with a handkerchief as his aides and fellow ministers surrounded him and the crowd rocked the temple with cheers and thunderous applause.

The following evening King was assassinated, shot in the head by a deranged racist, as he stood on the balcony of the Lorraine Motel. The civil rights movement, at least as he envisioned it, had drawn to a violent close.

Chapter 23

AMBUSH IN MERIDIAN

NINETEEN SIXTY-EIGHT was a year like no other. In addition to the shattering national and international events including the assassination of Robert Kennedy, the Tet Offensive in South Vietnam, and the riots across the country in the wake of Dr. King's murder, racial unrest continued to roil the South. I was still operating as a one-man band, madly dashing from protest march to court case to funeral procession. I didn't get home much that year, and when I did, I was usually on the phone. Telephone calls in the middle of the night were not unusual, but the one I got at 2 a.m. on June 30 started off memorably. "Okay, Jack, get your pencil out," ordered a booming voice. "We've got a big one this time, a goddamned big one. There's gonna be some wailing and gnashing of teeth."

It was Roy Gunn, police chief of Meridian, Mississippi calling about the Klan. A one-time defender of the KKK who had turned against it with a vengeance, he was an excitable man whose speech was laced with profanity interspersed with phrases from the Bible. Gunn picked me for the exclusive because he knew I had been covering the Klan intensively, and we had always gotten along well. The story—concerning a shootout between the Meridian police and two Klan members—was every bit as explosive as he promised. What I didn't know at the time was that many pieces were missing from his version. The complete story, which would not come to light for several months, was far more layered and even more explosive. It would cause me more sleepless nights than any case I had ever covered.

Even without possessing all the facts, I had one hell of an exclusive. "Police in Meridian, Mississippi, shot down a Ku Klux Klansman and his woman companion Sunday in a wild gun battle after the officers said the pair tried to dynamite a Jewish businessman's home," read my lead. I reported that the Klansman, a rabidly racist twenty-one-year-old named

Thomas Tarrants, was hit at least ten times with rifle and shotgun fire while emptying his submachine gun at policemen. He was still alive, but his companion, Kathy Ainsworth, a twenty-six-year-old schoolteacher, was killed. Two others, a police officer and a passerby, were seriously wounded. The police version, which I wrote, said the police were on the scene because they had been tipped off to the plan to firebomb the home of Meyer Davidson, a leading Meridian businessman. If the plan had gone off, it would have been the latest in a string of deadly attacks against Jewish targets in Mississippi.

At the time, the Klan was rampaging through the state, even though the FBI was bearing down hard on the KKK under orders from J. Edgar Hoover. He had no time for the civil rights movement, which he believed was riddled with Communists, but he could not permit domestic terrorists to run riot. The men in the lawmen's sights were not just any Klansmen. They were members of the secretive White Knights of the Ku Klux Klan, a breakaway group that favored violent action over talk. The organization had been founded by Sam Bowers, an eccentric fanatic, in 1964. At its peak, it had approximately six thousand members in Mississippi and was responsible for an estimated three hundred bombings, beatings, and burnings and at least nine murders.

With a few exceptions, the victims were black. But by 1967, Bowers and his followers had begun to turn their attention to Mississippi's Jews, a tiny community representing about 1.5 percent of the population. While adhering to their faith, Mississippi's Jews tended to blend in culturally, living lives of quiet comfort and prosperity. They were, in the main, descendants of assimilationist-minded German Jews who did not go in for public displays of their religion. It did not seem wise in a state where signs on the highway displayed slogans like "Are You Ready for Jesus?"

Their placid existence began to fray with the advent of the civil rights movement. The problem, from their point of view, was the number of Jews pouring in to take part in the Freedom Rides and demonstrations. By some estimates, 50 percent of the out-of-staters, mostly students, were Jewish, while 70 percent of the lawyers who lent aid to the movement were Jews.

There were few civil rights advocates among Jackson's Jewish community. The most conspicuous exception was its rabbi, Perry Nussbaum, who sympathized with the young demonstrators. Many of the students got arrested, and when the jails in Jackson got too full, they were thrown

into Parchman prison, a notorious hellhole 150 miles away. Rabbi Nussbaum knew he was courting danger, but he drove to Parchman once a
week to take the prisoners personal items like cigarettes and soap and to
collect notes to send to their families. Most of the congregation thought
the rabbi was endangering them. To some extent, they were right.

I had been reporting on the Klan in Mississippi for several years and
had closely followed the chain of anti-Semitic events that occurred prior
to the shoot-out in Meridian. On September 9, 1967, Jackson's newly
dedicated temple, Beth Israel, was dynamited late one night, heavily
damaging the structure. Two months later, Rabbi Nussbaum's house was
nearly destroyed while he and his wife were sleeping. Miraculously, they
escaped serious injury. The attacks provoked widespread expressions of
outrage and prompted a round-the-clock, all-hands-on-deck response
from law enforcement.

The response by the FBI and other police agencies in Mississippi to the
Jackson bombings was extraordinary, certainly by Mississippi standards.
For the most part, authorities had ignored the destruction of dozens of
black churches, most of the killings, and the brutalization of civil rights
workers. Exceptions included the massive manhunt for the killers of the
three young civil rights workers, Andrew Goodman, Michael Schwerner,
and James Chaney, on June 21, 1964, and the response to the murder of
Vernon Dahmer, an NAACP leader in Hattiesburg, who died when his
house was firebombed by the Klan on January 10, 1966.

Burning down black churches was one thing. Firebombing a synagogue and a rabbi's house proved to be another. Not only were the Jews
white; they were also well connected. Mississippi Senator James Eastland
let his good friend J. Edgar Hoover know that the attacks had to stop.
Agents were ordered to follow all known Klansmen for miles around,
interrogating them repeatedly and intimidating them in any way they
could. Every effort was made to develop informants, a nasty business
which might involve threatening to tell a wife about her husband's extra-
curricular dalliances if he didn't cooperate with the FBI. Still, no solid
leads to the identity of the Jackson bombers emerged.

Next on the list of the Klan's Jewish targets was the temple in Meridian, Mississippi, also called Beth Israel, where a powerful dynamite bomb
was set off on May 28, 1968. The blast blew out windows, shredded walls,
and opened a hole in the roof. Given the intensity of the investigations
and what I knew about the extensive use of informants, I was not surprised when I was told that police had been tipped off to the plan to

bomb Davidson's house. Nor did I delve deeply into how they found out. I was fascinated by the bomber, Tommy Tarrants, and his murdered companion, Kathy Ainsworth, and I followed up with long investigative profiles about them.

Originally from Mobile, Tarrants became involved in right-wing politics while still a teenager. A relative newcomer to the Jackson area, he didn't go in for sheets or rallies. He preferred operating alone. For a long time, he was known to the FBI simply as "The Man"; most members of the White Knights had never even heard of him. It wasn't until after the Meridian temple bombing that agents finally figured out his identity. An expert in explosives who could hit a plastic jug at one hundred yards, Tarrants was highly intelligent but lethal and hated Jews with an all-consuming passion.

His companion made good copy too. Kathy Ainsworth turned out to be a well-respected elementary school teacher by day and a committed terrorist at night. Pretty and seemingly sweet, she was married to a man who adored her, although he did not share her far-right views. There was a lot he didn't know about her. Few people, in fact, had any idea that she was learning how to make bombs and becoming proficient with weapons or that she had become romantically involved with Tarrants.

I also wrote about the murderous White Knights and their leader, Sam Bowers. The Imperial Wizard was a weird individual who sometimes wore a swastika and was seen clicking his heels and giving the Nazi salute in front of his old dog. He was regarded as an "unasylumed lunatic" by the FBI. Bowers had emerged, incorrectly, as it happened, as the chief suspect in the bombing of the temple and the rabbi's house. He was also believed to be the mastermind behind hundreds of racially motivated crimes in the state. But he was as wily as he was dangerous; the only conviction he received in the sixties was on federal civil rights charges in connection with the Philadelphia murders. Years later, in 1998, after numerous mistrials, he was sentenced to life in prison for ordering the 1966 death of Vernon Dahmer. Bowers died in the Mississippi State Penitentiary in 2006 at the age of eighty-two.

As with all the stories I did on the Klan—and I did a lot of them—I had substantial help from the FBI. I was in tight with many of the agents and regularly traded information with Roy Moore, the agent in charge of the 250-man Jackson office. I admired the bureau so much, in fact, that I found it hard to credit information I was getting that fall, suggesting that the FBI's role in the Meridian affair was questionable, to say the least.

The calls were coming from Ken Dean, a Baptist preacher and the director of the Mississippi Council on Human Relations. Dean's information was so explosive that he had consulted several friends, including Hodding Carter III, editor of the Greenville *Delta Democrat Times*, as to how to proceed. Carter suggested that I would be the best person to get the facts out.

Dean kept lines open to everybody in Mississippi, from Klansmen to cops, and his information was, in my experience, reliable. At first, his messages were cryptic. All he would tell me was that there was "a lot more to it." Then, in November, Dean finally got explicit. "You know they didn't expect to take them alive out there that night, don't you?" he said. "They paid somebody to get them to come out there. And they didn't expect Kathy Ainsworth to be in the car with Tarrants. They expected [local Klansman] Danny Joe Hawkins. You follow me?"

In essence he was telling me that the FBI and the police had concocted a deadly ambush and that the Jewish community had bankrolled the plot. I found the whole thing inconceivable, but I couldn't entirely dismiss what Dean was saying because he had never steered me wrong before. He said he was getting his information from A. I. (Bee) Botnick, the regional director of the Anti-Defamation League in New Orleans, a national organization charged with fighting discrimination against Jews. According to Dean, Botnick participated in formulating the plot. Botnick was also a good source of mine. He often phoned me with tips about the Klan. And Dean said Botnick's information was coming straight from the FBI.

It sounded so outlandish, I thought I would be wasting my time. Furthermore, there was a part of me that didn't want to believe the story was true, so high was my regard for the FBI. But after persistent prodding from Dean, I telephoned Botnick at his office. When I told him what I'd heard, there was a long silence on the other end of the phone. Finally, he confirmed that Tarrants, and, unwittingly, Ainsworth had been lured into a trap by a pair of informants and that the Jewish community had put up the money to pay them. But he said he could not "morally blow the whistle on the FBI" because they had stopped the violence. What he said was true. Since the ambush, there had been no further violence against Jews in Mississippi.

Even then, I didn't jump on the story despite more prodding from Ken Dean, who was by now obsessed with the case. Aside from the press of daily news, in 1969 I was busy working on a book with Jack Bass about the Orangeburg massacre, which had taken place the previous year. Finally, that fall, Dean came to my office in Atlanta with an eleven-page, single-spaced typed memo, outlining what he knew. It was so precise and detailed that my heart sank. For an investigative reporter with an inside track to the bureau like me, pursuing the story meant burning some important bridges. The FBI, I knew, would cut me off. On a personal level, I genuinely liked the people I would be putting in a bad light. I had great respect for Botnick and Gunn, and I considered Roy Moore, the special agent in charge of the Jackson office, a personal friend. By now, however, I realized that whether or not all of Dean's assertions checked out, it was clear that an abuse of police power had taken place. I felt the public had a right to know about it and judge the bureau's actions for themselves.

My next call was to Chief Gunn in Jackson. I told him I was working on a follow-up story to the shoot-out, which pleased him. He, like others on the force, felt the police had never gotten the credit they deserved. He suggested that I talk to Luke Scarborough, a Meridian detective who had been in on the plot from the start. He had worked closely with the FBI to cultivate the informants and bend them to their will.

I hit pay dirt with Scarborough. "Hell, this is a story Hollywood couldn't make up," he said, as I got a tape recorder rolling in my motel room in Jackson. He was eager to cooperate because he felt he never got the credit he deserved for the major role he had played. He even offered to show me a stack of documents. The catch was he wanted to be paid. I had never before paid for information, but I reasoned that this case was different. We wouldn't be paying for an interview. We would be paying for documents, the most trustworthy form of information.

After I talked it over with our national editor Ed Guthman, we decided to offer Scarborough one thousand dollars, a large sum for a small-town detective in those days. He delivered the documents in a folder later that afternoon and let me borrow them so I could go out and copy them. I pretended to stroll out of the room casually, but as soon as I was out of sight, I ran the four blocks to a law office where I knew I could use the copying machine. It was all there in the folder—official documents neatly typed and dated, with precise details, telling how the money was raised and how the lawmen dealt with the two informants—brothers and bullyboys named Alton Wayne and Raymond Roberts. The documents also spelled out how, at the FBI's urging, the brothers persuaded Tommy Tarrants and his usual partner in crime, Danny Joe Hawkins, to dynamite a Jewish businessman's house in Meridian.

Over the course of the next two days, Scarborough poured out the details of the plot. The police were anticipating a shoot-out, he said. They knew that Tarrants and Hawkins would be heavily armed, and they did not expect to take either of them alive. Nor did they expect Tarrants to show up with a woman. Nobody knew until the last minute that Kathy Ainsworth had substituted for Hawkins, deeply disturbing the assembled marksmen waiting in the bushes around Davidson's house.

Scarborough's account of his dealings with the Roberts brothers was hair-raising. Night after night, until two, three, four o'clock in the morning, he and FBI agents Frank Watts and Jack Rucker met with the brothers in a lonely trailer outside of town, trying to get their cooperation. The carrot they held out was money: the Jews of Jackson had put up eighty-five thousand dollars to pay for informants to set the plot in motion. (The Roberts brothers only received thirty-six thousand dollars in the end.) The stick: escalating threats by the local police and the FBI to kill them if they didn't cooperate.

Scarborough recounted an early meeting when everybody present put their guns on the table. Next to the guns, he counted out a down payment of one thousand dollars in stacks of twenty-dollar bills. Agent Frank Watts looked at the Klansmen, then pointed to the money. "Over here," he said, "you've got money coming in." Then he pointed to the guns. "Or over here you can have your ass shot off one night when you come out here. It's your choice. We expect your cooperation."

A combination of greed and fear finally won the brothers over. They cooked up a story, telling Tarrants and Hawkins that Alton Wayne, a suspect in the temple bombings, needed help to throw police off the scent. The idea was for Tarrants and Hawkins to strike at a Jewish target in Meridian, making sure that Alton Wayne was seen carousing at a nightclub in Jackson, giving him an airtight alibi. The hit men bought it.

Although I didn't let on, Scarborough's recitation deeply shocked me. I knew the FBI could play rough, but threatening to kill people who refused to cooperate? Setting up death traps? Later I discovered that at least some of the tactics came straight from an FBI playbook known as COINTELPRO, a secret domestic counterintelligence program first used against Communists in the fifties. As a later Senate investigation would document, COINTELPRO often used illegal methods to disrupt, discredit, and sow discord among targeted groups such as the Socialist Workers Party, the Black Panthers, the antiwar left, and the Klan.

Tactics included planting phony reports in the news media, smearing people through forgeries, wrongful imprisonment, blackmail, and sending poison-pen letters to try to break up marriages. Secrecy was paramount, because public exposure of such dirty tricks would be deeply embarrassing to the bureau.

Agents in the South were urged to develop "compromise data on immorality, dishonesty, and devious tactics" which could be used to force Klansmen to cooperate or to promote distrust among the various Klan units. They made use of reporters too, including me. Frequently my stories were based on information specifically supplied by FBI sources to let the Klan know that the FBI knew what they were up to and to keep them nervous about infiltrators in their ranks. It was psychological warfare pushed to the limit—and beyond—of the law.

My profile of Sam Bowers is an example of my close cooperation with the FBI. The bureau gave me his history—where he went to school, his family background, and so on. Some of the information I developed on my own—I found Bowers's mother in Mobile, for example—but there's no doubt that I could write a story faster and better when the FBI was supplying me with background. This was another instance where I was unwittingly serving as an arm of the law, and I don't recall that I had any qualms at the time about how my work was being used. In retrospect I realize I ought not to have been helping the FBI do its job, particularly when it involved abuses of power, but at the time, I didn't see the harm in it. In fact, I thought I was performing a service.

The Meridian story would pull back the curtain to some extent on COINTELPRO, although the name of the program would not be revealed until the mid-1970s. The sensitivity of the story had Guthman and me so worried that we decided I needed another reporter present when conducting further interviews. Guthman sent Nick Chriss of our Houston bureau to back me up. Nick and I paid an unannounced visit to Bee Botnick in New Orleans, who was obviously having second thoughts about what he had told me. Suddenly, he couldn't remember anything, even when I read back his remarks from the transcript of our interview. As we left his office, Chriss said to me, "You do what you gotta do, but you'll never get anything out of old Bee Botnick again."

It was time to pay a call on the FBI's Roy Moore, which I'd been dreading. When I told him what I knew and that I had the records to back it up, he looked shocked that I would even consider writing a story that raised the question of entrapment. (I didn't have the heart at this point to question him about the matter of the prearranged ambush.) In any event, he insisted the FBI had only played a minimal role in the whole affair. As for the question of the Jews raising money to pay the Roberts brothers, he said, "If you knew everything that occurred leading up to the Meridian shoot-out, you would feel that the Jewish community should be commended for the part it played in raising funds for the informants because they supplied the wherewithal for it and it saved their people's lives."

Moore was not being overly dramatic. One of the pivotal events that galvanized the Jews of Jackson to put up the money was the existence of a chilling recording of a conversation between two Klansmen which the FBI played for Jewish leaders. On it, one Klansman proposed planting a firebomb in the temple's air-conditioning system, attached to a timing device that would set off the firebomb at a time when the synagogue would be full of people. The other Klansman sounded horrified, pointing out that the explosion would kill children. "The hell with that," the first man declared. "Little Jew bastards grow up to be big Jew devils. Kill 'em while they're young."

I knew about this tape as well as the tepid expressions of support Jackson's Jews got after the bombings from the town's business pillars, most of its religious leaders, and the segregationist *Jackson Daily News*. What would I have done if I was in their position, I asked myself. There was no easy answer. Thinking about a similar threat involving my own three children, I realized I might have done the same thing. How could I criticize others when they seemingly had no recourse?

Moore pulled out every argument he could think of to dissuade me from going ahead with the investigation. "If you write the story," he warned, "the blood of innocent people will be on your hands. It will yank the rug from under our law enforcement program in Mississippi." My stomach was in knots by the time we left his office. It wasn't just the knowledge that I had alienated the ADL and the FBI, probably forever. It was also what Moore had said about the blood of innocent people and undermining law enforcement. I, who usually fall asleep as soon as I hit the bed, began to endure sleepless nights and stomach-churning days. To add to my anguish, I got a registered letter from Detective Luke Scarborough containing the thousand-dollar check from the *Los Angeles Times*.

"Jack," he wrote, "I told you at the start I would never name any informers or other people who were involved. You are writing about vicious, bloodthirsty Klansmen who are waiting for certain names to be made public and there will be retaliation by them. This blood will be on your hands and your conscience."

In fact, by then, just about everyone in Jackson had figured out that the Roberts brothers were the informants. Despite being warned repeatedly by the FBI to keep a low profile, each of them bought a fancy new car, and they went around town flashing rolls of bills. Scarborough called them a pair of idiots. But he finished his letter to me with a warning I couldn't ignore. "You are a high-classed writer with a good reputation and I hope you won't let one story ruin your future. You know, being transferred to Washington, D.C., a good reputation will mean a lot to you."

Scarborough was alluding to the move I was about to make to the Washington bureau of the *L.A. Times*. I could see Roy Moore's handiwork in the letter, and it made me shiver. If the FBI set out to ruin my reputation, I knew it would unquestionably cause me a lot of harm. But I continued to work on the story while bracing for the fallout I knew was coming.

In the ensuing months, I traveled and did numerous follow-ups on the shoot-out, including Tarrants's trial, incarceration, escape from prison, and recapture. In another remarkable twist, the one-time mad-dog bomber converted to Christianity, and, with the backing of FBI agent Watts and Al Binder, a prominent member of Jackson's Jewish community, he was released from prison after serving eight years. He went on to marry a wealthy woman and become an ordained minister.

I kept tabs on all the twists and turns, and eventually, I would write a book about the affair called *Terror in the Night: The Klan's Campaign Against the Jews*. Possibly because it took such a toll on me emotionally, this was the one case in which I saved every shred of paper, every tape recording, every note I took. But I wouldn't get around to writing the book until the nineties. Well before that, I had to deal with a more immediate effect of my reporting after I got to Washington: a smear campaign launched by J. Edgar Hoover.

Chapter 24

NUMBER ONE ON J. EDGAR HOOVER'S SHIT LIST

I CAME UP FROM ATLANTA on my own. My three teenage children adamantly refused to move; the boys even threatened to run away if I tried to force them to part with their friends. Virginia didn't want to move either. The truth is, our marriage was badly frayed by then. How could it have been otherwise when I was often putting in as many as twenty-five days a month on the road. Nevertheless, she and I remained married for four more years, and I continued to send home most of my earnings. This meant that I was living on pretty short rations. I recall attending a lot of cocktail parties and receptions on the Hill where I could stoke up on the free food and booze. For company, I hung out nearly every night at Tammany Hall, a bar on Pennsylvania Avenue frequented by newspaper people and politicians and where an unknown singer named Emmylou Harris used to perform. When Tammany closed, we all migrated to the Class Reunion, a convivial place on H Street, not far from the White House.

I often shut the place down and no doubt drank more than was good for me. But I was always sitting at my desk at 9 a.m. in suit and tie, hard at work no matter how much I'd had to drink the night before. (A line about the Class Reunion eventually made its way onto the TV show *Lou Grant*. Seems one of the writers had heard the story, which actually happened, about *Times* managing editor Frank Haven looking at my expense account one day and loudly complaining, "Why in the hell are we always paying for Nelson to go to his class reunions?")

I was still moving into my new apartment in Washington when the Meridian story ran on February 13, 1970. My six-thousand-word account was splashed across the front page of the *L.A. Times*, while the *Washington Post* ran it as a series of three front-page articles. In an eloquent lead editorial, the *Times* described the events in Meridian as "most painful and disturbing," declaring that the authorities had stretched the law to unacceptable limits. "No matter how great the provocation, the police can never take it on themselves to decide who is guilty, who is innocent; who is to live, and who to die." Although the American Civil Liberties Union and the American Friends Service Committee both called for an official investigation, the affair was quickly forgotten outside of Mississippi, mainly because of the tsunami of competing news events.

The FBI did not forget. I was already unpopular with the bureau and Hoover because of an episode that occurred in the wake of Martin Luther King Jr.'s assassination, when Nick Chriss and I managed to get to some of the witnesses before the FBI did. *Life* magazine mentioned it, causing embarrassment at the bureau. When my colleague Ron Ostrow called the FBI for comment on another matter, he was told by Tom Bishop, who headed up the PR shop, that Chriss and I had been going around with liquor on our breaths questioning witnesses and fouling up the FBI's investigation.

The Meridian story launched a fusillade of derogatory memos within the FBI, which I would later obtain, in heavily edited form, under the Freedom of Information Act. In response to a memo from Roy Moore, Hoover scrawled on it, "Our Jackson Office should be more circumspect with Nelson as any representative of the L.A. Times can't be trusted. H." (Hoover used to write brusque comments on memos and sign them "H.") On another internal memo he scribbled, "It is obvious now that Nelson played Moore for a sucker." He got more apoplectic as time went by, giving instructions at the bottom of another memo: "This jackal Nelson is to be given nothing." On another he called me "a lice-covered ferret."

The FBI flatly denied playing a part in setting up the ambush or investigating the shootings. So did the ADL. In a statement, the Jewish organization maintained it had no part "in the disbursement of funds nor any contact with informants nor any participation in the police activity." Bee Botnick, not surprisingly, was furious with me. It got back to me that he was saying I was "dead" in my profession—that the ADL was making use of its contacts in government and industry to dry up my news sources. I didn't believe that Botnick could do me that much harm, but I was not happy to hear that he was going around talking that way.

Chief Roy Gunn maintained a defiant stance. "I owe no apologies to anyone and should the same thing occur again it is possible the same method would be used. This is a police matter in which my department learned in advance of the plans of the Ku Klux Klan to commit murder. . . . There was nothing illegal or unethical about the method that my department used to prevent these murders."

Gunn went on to attack me personally. He told reporters that Klan informants advised him that my real purpose in writing the story was to "discredit my police department and the FBI and actually remove Mr. Hoover, who they believed had set himself up as a czar. This apparently is a left-wing group that does not want law enforcement."

I was certain that Hoover was the driving force behind Gunn's comments, which were aimed at the *Los Angeles Times* as well as at me. One memo I obtained describes how the agent in charge of the Los Angeles office, Wesley Grapp, was "reminded" by headquarters that cooperation with the *Times* was to cease. Grapp needed no persuading. He is quoted in the memo as calling the paper a "melting pot of garbage," and stating that the paper "daily prints false stories concerning people in public life. It makes no difference to this paper whether the stories are true or not." Grapp also said he thought the *Times* would print anything if it thought it would be damaging to the FBI.

When the FBI captured black political activist Angela Davis, one of the bureau's ten most wanted fugitives, on October 13, 1970, the *Times*, alone among major papers, was not notified. The next day, when bureau chief Dave Kraslow called Tom Bishop, who ran the bureau's public relations operation, he got an earful. "When you get rid of that son of a bitch with a vendetta against the FBI, we'll cooperate with you," Bishop shouted into the phone. Bishop went on to tell Kraslow that I had gotten drunk and gone around town telling people I was going to "get" Hoover and the FBI.

There is no telling how many people heard the same scurrilous lies. I do know that when Bill Eaton of the *Chicago Daily News* called Bishop for a comment on allegations about the FBI in *The Orangeburg Massacre*, Bishop told him that I drank too much and could not be believed. Eaton told me Bishop referred to me as "that drunk" and said I was "number one on J. Edgar Hoover's shit list."

I was not deterred. If anything I bore down harder, because my investigations in the South had convinced me that both Hoover and the FBI reeked of corruption. It's true that in the early days Hoover had amassed a sterling record, taking a moribund agency and building it into a modern, effective crime-fighting organization. His well-publicized exploits—nabbing bank robbers and gangsters like John Dillinger and Machine Gun Kelly, and capturing spies and saboteurs during World War II—were lapped up by an adoring public. But he had been reigning over law enforcement since 1924, and Lord Acton's famous dictum about power corrupting and absolute power corrupting absolutely was never truer than when applied to Hoover.

When I got to Washington, Hoover was still a sacrosanct figure. He had inoculated himself against criticism from elected officials—they were too frightened to cross him. And as far as I could tell, my colleague Ron Ostrow, who had unparalleled sources in the Justice Department, myself, and Jack Anderson were the only journalists doing any sustained reporting on abuses at the bureau at that time. I suppose I took on the FBI as a special project, which is ironic in view of my long-standing hero worship of J. Edgar Hoover. I remember how honored Virginia and I felt in 1960 to get a VIP tour of the FBI during a trip to Washington. There's a memo in my voluminous file stating that "Nelson is a strong supporter of the Bureau and above all desires, while in Washington to have a tour of our headquarters." A follow-up memo, describing the tour in detail, made mention of the fact that I asked for and received some empty shells and a target from the firearms range to take home to my kids. "[Nelson] stated that he and his wife enjoyed the tour of the FBI more than anything they had done in a long time. He stated it was the finest sight in Washington."

Once my eyes were opened by the events in Meridian, I began hammering away at the FBI the way I'd pounded on the Griffin administration in Georgia in the fifties. I often worked with Ron Ostrow, and we painted a picture of a man who had little in common with the image of demigod so carefully fashioned by the FBI over the years. Our Hoover was a chiseling, vindictive autocrat who treated FBI personnel as if they were his errand boys. Agents had to contribute to elaborate gifts which were presented to the director four times a year—Christmas, his birthday, the anniversary of his joining the Justice Department, and the anniversary of his becoming director of the FBI. One Christmas, employees built a mahogany pirate's chest with brass hinges and latches and put in a case of Jack Daniel's Black Label. He had bureau staffers put air-conditioning in his house and build him a porch, all on government time.

We disclosed that he got a new thirty-thousand-dollar armor-plated Cadillac each year (compared with the president of the United States who had to make do with a five-thousand-dollar leased limousine). The old model would be assigned to another FBI office, usually in areas where Hoover liked to vacation, thus building up a fleet around the nation. His car had to be impeccable or heads would roll. Once one of his tires blew out during a trip to Pennsylvania; thereafter, the Caddy had to be equipped with a new set of tires every time he went on the road.

More serious were the lengths to which Hoover and his FBI would go to secure convictions, often relying on information from the most unsavory sources. Ron and I uncovered a number of these individuals, including at least one agent provocateur: Robert William Hardy, the chief government witness against a group that raided a draft board in Camden, New Jersey. "[The raid] definitely wouldn't have happened without me," Hardy said in an affidavit. "I provided 90 percent of the tools necessary for the action. . . . It included hammers, ropes, drills, and bits. They couldn't use some of the tools without hurting themselves, so I taught them."

No one could have been sleazier than Boyd Frederick Douglas, a convict who informed against a prominent group of antiwar Catholic activists, including Father Philip Berrigan. Acting on suspicions by members of the group, Ron and I were able to report that the informer was a three-time felon with convictions for forging checks, auto theft, assaulting an FBI agent, impersonating an army officer, and five escapes or attempted escapes from prison.

Not surprisingly, when the case went to trial, the defense was able to shred Douglas's credibility, and the government was unable to prove a conspiracy existed. (The jury took nearly seven days to reach a verdict, which was finally delivered on April 7, 1972, and it was while hanging around the jury room for hours on end that I met my wife-to-be, Barbara Matusow, who was covering the tail end of the trial for *CBS Radio News*.) Ron and I later wrote a book about the affair called *The FBI and the Berrigans*, in which we concluded that the case would never have been tried but for Hoover, who was seeking vindication for earlier rash charges he had made against Philip and his brother, Daniel.

The story I wrote that kicked up the biggest storm delved into the plight of an FBI agent named Jack Shaw. A thirty-seven-year-old former marine captain with a spotless record who'd served seven years with the bureau, Shaw was studying for a master's degree at John Jay College of Criminal Justice in New York. Seeking advice about his thesis, he wrote what he thought was a private letter to one of his professors, discussing what he saw as the strengths and weaknesses of the FBI. One the negative side, he wrote that the personality cult surrounding Hoover stymied change at the FBI. He also criticized it for laxity in pursuing organized crime and for regimenting agents too severely. On the plus side, he defended Hoover's integrity and character and wrote that, overall, the FBI was providing effective law enforcement.

Shaw turned the fifteen-page single-spaced letter over to the typing pool, and the next thing he knew, agents were rooting through the school's trash baskets, piecing together what he'd written. The following day he was suspended without pay for thirty days, put on probation, and transferred to Butte, Montana, an outpost to which agents who displeased the director were exiled. Shaw, the father of four whose wife was ill and did not have long to live, opted to resign. Hoover accepted his resignation "with prejudice," which effectively barred Shaw from future employment in law enforcement. When Shaw realized his predicament, he wrote to Hoover requesting that the black mark be removed from his record. Hoover refused.

My account of Shaw's firing and follow-up stories got big play around the country, prompting Senator George McGovern to call for a congressional investigation. An incensed Hoover went into damage control mode, prompting a dozen top bureau officials to write McGovern scathing letters. But McGovern surprised them by going public with the letters. Suddenly, other congressmen began speaking out. Representative Hale Boggs said on the House floor that the FBI had been tapping his phone. He called the bureau a "secret police" that compiled dossiers on innocent people and called for Hoover's resignation. Senator Edmund Muskie rose to denounce the FBI's snooping on Earth Day activities. These were shocking developments; no one of comparable stature had dared to criticize Hoover for years up to this time. But to my intense chagrin, the *Los Angeles Times* was beginning to ignore or play down what I thought were significant developments regarding the FBI, even though other newspapers were getting into the act.

In a long, anguished and somewhat rambling letter to my boss and good friend Ed Guthman, dated April 6, 1971, I complained bitterly about the way Los Angeles was downplaying our stories—or not playing them at all.

> I thought it was pertinent that [Senator] John Tunney was applauded for his comment about FBI dossiers in Columbia, South Carolina. The *New York Times* used it and also played the Boggs story on page one. The *Washington Post* played [the Boggs story] on page one—the *Washington Star* bannered it yesterday. I realize that we don't go by what other papers do and you may think we're using good judgment. I just happen to disagree. When Hale

Boggs calls for Hoover's dismissal—not retirement—and refers to the FBI as using gestapo tactics, I think that's big news. When he does it in the aftermath of stories we have broken about the FBI using agents provocateur and engaging in other highly questionable activities, it seems to me we ought to consider it even bigger news.

The *New York Times* has run two editorials calling for an investigation of Hoover and the FBI. Their editorials were based mainly on stories the *L.A. Times* has broken. The *Cleveland Plain Dealer* and other papers that carried our Shaw story followed it with editorials calling for an investigation and/or Hoover's resignation. Again, I know we should not be influenced one way or the other by the editorial page. . . . But I think it's fair for me to assume that there isn't much enthusiasm by the *L.A. Times* to make the hard decision to devote whatever time and effort is necessary to report the whole truth about the FBI and to tell our readers that we believe it is a corrupt institution directed by a corrupt man.

I know I haven't told you anything new, Ed, but you must know by now that despite the fact the *L.A. Times* has done more than any other paper and has been quite lenient with me concerning the FBI, I still feel somewhat constrained in this area . . . After all, you told me I would be pretty free to do what I thought ought to be done. And you've lived up to that as I knew you would. But right now I still see the FBI and the Berrigan case as being two major stories that I can't turn loose. And both still need a lot of investigating. I hope I'll continue to be free to do that.

By now, I was in a highly emotional state. I even considered quitting the paper when Ron and I were called off a story involving a top FBI official close to the White House. The FBI man's mortgage was being paid by a businessman, and to make the arrangement even fishier, the businessman sought and received an appointment as a roving ambassador from the president. We, of course, wanted to press ahead with our investigation, but editors were swayed by the FBI's pleas that the official was about to retire and faced financing the college tuitions of several children.

I was seething; I could not recall anything like this happening to me before. I was in such a rage that Ron urged me to go outside and get some air. The two of us walked around the block about a dozen times while I vented my fury. At the time, the *New York Times* was sounding me out about a job, and much as I loved the *L.A. Times*, the prospect was beginning to sound attractive. In the end, I decided to stay where I was, but I continued to chafe at the way my stories were being played.

During this period, Ed was doing his best to calm me down and run interference with some of the more conservative editors on the paper. But he made it plain that he would prefer to see me turn my attention to matters other than the FBI.

> Jack [he wrote], I don't think we repeatedly have to demonstrate either our interest in your FBI work or our willingness to publish what you find out. I am concerned only that we do not appear to be carping at the bureau. If that happens, we will be defeating our purpose and reducing our credibility with our readers. I believe this about investigative reporting whether it's J. Edgar Hoover or Sam Yorty or the Harbor Commission. A paper can be made to appear to be harassing a public official.
>
> . . . I want to avoid that if I can. Investigating the FBI and covering the Berrigan case are exceptionally sensitive and emotional subjects. I'm counting on you to keep your balance and it isn't going to be easy. We expect you to follow the trail wherever it leads. We're prepared to print what you find out. But we're not gong to nitpick or muckrake.

Then he got to the nub of the matter:

> I do hope that you'll have some time and opportunity to constantly broaden your knowledge of Washington. It's my long-range hope that you'll acquire working knowledge of what's behind most of the big doors and develop the sources to find out what is going on with respect to public policy as well as corruption and malfeasance. . . . End of sermon. All the best, Ed

For a tough, one-time investigative reporter like Ed to back off a story was deeply unsettling to me. Yet he was in a tight spot, and we both knew it. The problem was that he had been close to Robert Kennedy and had served as his press secretary at the Justice Department. Hoover, as was well known, despised Bobby Kennedy; the two men had barely been on speaking terms. So Guthman was presumed to be an enemy too.

There are several derogatory references to Ed in my file, including one dated February 23, 1970, that shocked me—from Clark Mollenhof of all people, the man who had done me such a good turn years earlier. He was then briefly serving as special counsel to Richard Nixon's White House and in a transparent attempt to curry favor with Hoover, Mollenhof sent Hoover a memo saying I was planning a highly critical series on the FBI. "This reporter is very persistent and will undoubtedly be influenced to some degree by the strong anti-FBI views of Ed Guthman, national editor of the Los Angeles Times," he wrote. At the bottom of the memo, Hoover scrawled, "Good. Keep an eye on these characters. They are up to no good."

Ed acknowledged that his Kennedy associations were not helping my case. "In connection with the FBI," he wrote to me, "we are particularly vulnerable to the charge that there is something personal about what you are doing (more because of me than because of you). So, if I appear overly cautious to you, well, you know the reason."

Guthman wasn't the only Los Angeles Times man feeling heat from the FBI. Publisher Otis Chandler was too liberal for Hoover's taste, as was our no-holds-barred cartoonist Paul Conrad. A memo dated March 24, 1970, addressed to Tom Bishop states, "Our files reveal that since the early 1960's [when Otis became publisher] this newspaper has taken the opportunity to criticize us, either in editorials or cartoons, on a number of occasions, and it has been necessary for [Special Agent in Charge Wesley] Grapp to contact and straighten out representatives of this newspaper."

In an effort to improve relations, Robert Nelson (no relation), executive vice president and general manager of the Times, traveled to Washington to meet with Hoover on October 1, 1971. In preparation for the meeting, an eight-page, single-spaced memorandum was compiled for the director, summarizing my history with the FBI. When I later obtained the memo, I was shocked to find it filled with erroneous and defamatory information from informants who were either anonymous or whose names had been blacked out. For example: "The numerous references in our files on Jack Nelson clearly identify him to us as an individual with a deep-seated hatred of the FBI. He has written numerous articles criticizing the Director and the Bureau . . . During January, 1970, Nelson allegedly stated that he was associated with 'a group' which had as its purpose 'a nationwide move to remove J. Edgar Hoover, the head of the FBI, who has set himself up as a Czar.'"

There was one baseless allegation that seemed to agitate Hoover more than any other. An informant was quoted as saying that after having several drinks at a symposium, I told him and others that I had documentation that Hoover was a homosexual and that I planned to write an article about it.

What Robert Nelson made of these charges I don't know, but the extent of Hoover's concern on the subject would soon become clear. Two weeks after the meeting with Robert Nelson, on October 13, 1971, bureau chief Dave Kraslow sat down with Hoover, and he raised the subject several times. After the meeting, which lasted nearly two hours, Kraslow came back to the bureau and dictated a long, stream-of-consciousness memo. In it, he described the director sitting behind his desk in a large red leather chair, reading almost nonstop from a pile of documents.

"The rapidity with which he spoke was an indication of his agitation," wrote Kraslow. "He was intense. It was quite evident that he was upset, particularly on the question of the homosexual charge . . . The question came up several times in the conversation, and each time more heatedly than the previous time. And at one point Hoover said he recognized that a paper as reputable as the *Los Angeles Times* would never print such an allegation, and if they did, of course he would sue for criminal slander. And he said he didn't want this to be considered a threat, but if it came to his attention that Jack ever again made some remark about Hoover being a homosexual, he would sue Jack for criminal slander. . . ."

Kraslow noted that Hoover repeated himself several times, and he was constantly getting names mixed up, several times referring to "Jack Anderson" when he was talking about me. He would catch himself, but he said he thought of us both in the same vein, and that we were both no good. In addition to denouncing my reporting on Orangeburg, Meridian, and the Berrigan case, Hoover listed many of the same offenses he outlined for Robert Nelson—my "excessive" drinking, my "sick" attitude towards the FBI, my claim that I had been assigned to the Washington bureau for the express purpose of "getting" him, my saying I was so hung up on the FBI I had become "paranoid."

Several times Kraslow was forced to interrupt Hoover in order to defend me, telling him that none of his allegations accorded in the slightest with what he knew about me. Hoover responded by saying that I had a Jekyll-Hyde personality, and that when I was under the influence of alcohol, I became a different person.

Kraslow suggested that it might help if Hoover were to meet with me—I had in fact repeatedly sought to interview him, even showing up at his office unannounced—but Hoover told Kraslow he wasn't interested. "He said he had learned a long time ago not to get into a pissing contest with a skunk, that there was no percentage, that he could not win, that he had no intention of meeting Jack."

At the end of the meeting, Kraslow concluded, "I think Hoover accepted the fact, as I did, that we left on a basis where we had irreconcilable differences of opinion about Jack Nelson."

I was floored when Kraslow relayed Hoover's charges to me. I had never even remotely suggested that he was a homosexual, and there was never any talk about a campaign to "get" him. And no one who knew me would have considered me a drunk. I was so upset I even offered to take a lie detector test, but Kraslow found the idea repugnant. Instead, I sat down and wrote a letter to Hoover, explicitly denying every one of his allegations, including the one about heavy drinking. I wrote, "You allege that I am well known in Washington as an excessive drinker and that I have a Jekyll and Hyde personality. . . . I deny that I am a drunk or that I am well known in Washington as an excessive drinker or that I had alcohol on my breath when interviewing witnesses in the King case. I deny the allegation of insanity—that I have a Jekyll and Hyde personality. I would be interested in meeting face to face with any of your alleged informants on the questions of drinking and a split personality—or on any other subject, for that matter. Those are serious charges for the director of the FBI to level against a man in a conversation with his employer."

I requested that my letter be made part of my dossier, and Kraslow wrote a firm letter to Hoover defending me. In it he said, "You have never met Mr. Nelson. I have known him for ten years as a competent professional and a man of honor. When I weigh that knowledge and his statements to me against the alleged assertions of faceless accusers, I am compelled to only one conclusion. I must accept Mr. Nelson's word, and I know from experience that his word is good."

It was gratifying to know I had the backing of my bosses, but as it turned out, I would not be investigating the FBI much longer. On May 2, 1972, J. Edgar Hoover died, and his successor, Clarence Kelly, ushered in a new era of openness and cooperation with the press. Although he and I developed a good working relationship, in a few months I would be consumed with investigating the scandal of the century: Watergate.

Editor's Note

—BARBARA MATUSOW

The story of my husband's life ends abruptly for the sad reason that he died before he had a chance to finish writing it. Jack passed away on October 21, 2009, at the age of eighty, after a losing bout with pancreatic cancer. He always intended that the memoir he was writing would encompass his years in Washington, where he served as the high-profile bureau chief of the *Los Angeles Times* for twenty-one years. That, alas, was not to be. But he did leave behind a vivid account of his youth and his trail-blazing career as a reporter in the South.

The manuscript was not a finished work—many chapters were polished to a high gloss, others not. There were holes in the story here and there. Was it publishable if the gaps could be filled and the rough spots smoothed? I wondered. I didn't know. Fortunately, I was able to turn for advice to *the* experts in the field of southern journalism—Eugene Roberts and Hank Klibanoff, coauthors of the Pulitzer Prize–winning *The Race Beat: The Press, the Civil Rights Struggle, and the Awakening of a Nation.*

Their verdict was unambiguous: the manuscript could and should be published, even in its truncated form. Happily, the editors at the University Press of Mississippi, along with veteran southern journalist Curtis Wilkie, concurred, although everyone agreed that the book needed work.

Initially I was not interested in taking on the job, even though in many respects I was the obvious person. I had a long career in journalism, first as a radio and television reporter and producer, then as longtime staff writer for *Washingtonian* magazine. As a close couple, both personally and professionally, Jack and I read and critiqued each other's work throughout our thirty-five-year marriage. We even met on the job.

In early 1972, Jack was in Harrisburg, Pennsylvania, covering the trial of the so-called Harrisburg Seven, the Catholic activists charged with attempting to kidnap Henry Kissinger. I, an inexperienced reporter in New York for *CBS News*, was sent to Harrisburg towards the end of the trial to handle radio feeds once the verdict was in. Jury stakeouts of this kind can last for days, with dozens of reporters milling about killing time—reading, kibitzing, doing crossword puzzles, etc. That's when I first encountered the great Jack Nelson, already famous in journalistic circles for his investigative prowess and his coverage of civil rights.

After several days of deliberation, the jury finally came back. Apart from some minor charges of letter smuggling, members were hopelessly deadlocked on all the serious counts. The jurors, who weren't talking to reporters, proceeded to disperse into the Pennsylvania countryside. It was our job to track them down for comment. Not knowing where to begin, I was on the verge of panic. But Jack, always generous with fellow reporters, gave me the names and addresses of several jurors. I was so grateful for his help that our casual friendship quickly morphed into romance. Two years and many trips between New York and Washington later, we were married.

We were the closest of collaborators throughout our marriage. I never turned in a magazine article without showing it to him first, and he always asked me to edit the lengthier pieces he was working on. I also served as a legman on his 1991 book, *Terror in the Night: The Klan's Campaign Against the Jews*, taking a leave of absence from my magazine job to conduct interviews and do research. But for some unknown reason, I resisted getting involved in his memoir. After he died, I was no more enthusiastic, even thinking of hiring someone to finish the book. But I was pretty sure that wouldn't work.

The principal deterrent, as far as I was concerned, was his papers. I knew they were absolutely crucial if I were to finish the task. But they were in a grave state of disorganization, which is to say, they were barely organized at all. The thought of sorting and cataloging fifteen file boxes stuffed with fifty years' worth of notes, tapes, letters, memorabilia, etc., filled me with dread. Yet I knew I owed it to his memory to do what I could to get his story out, and in order to accomplish this, I would have to attack his papers.

As I began going through and filing them, instead of the drudgery I had anticipated, the search turned out to be more like a treasure hunt. I kept finding gems—letters, interviews, articles about Jack, articles by Jack, oral histories, speeches, etc.—that would enable me to fill in the gaps. Best of all, for the most part I would be able to use his own words. In writing about how he broke the story of a police-protected lottery ring in Atlanta in the fifties, for example, he didn't mention in his draft the threats and harassment he and his family suffered in the aftermath. But there it was in a memorandum he wrote in 1991—the anonymous calls in the middle of the night, the police descending on his house with drawn pistols, the fire engines screeching up at all hours.

Letters were another mother lode. In one anguished exchange with his editor at the *Los Angeles Times,* he complained bitterly about the way his FBI exclusives were being downplayed, evidently in response to pressure from J. Edgar Hoover. As my discoveries mounted, I could scarcely pass the room where I was working without going in and delving further. (Happily, the papers now reside in the outstanding collection of all matters southern at Emory University.)

When it came time to insert the material, I found the job immensely satisfying, even invigorating. My only regret was that I hadn't helped Jack, who was singularly averse to filing *anything*, organize his papers while he was alive. Somehow, though, he managed to find enough or remember enough to create an engaging, significant account of his incandescent career. It was my privilege to help him finish the task.

People often asked if it was uncomfortable or sad for me to work on Jack's book. My answer was and remains the same. It was a labor of love.

Epilogue: The Washington Years

—RICHARD T. COOPER

I first met Jack on a hectic street corner in Chicago at the 1968 Democratic National Convention—the new guy in the midwest bureau respectfully shaking hands with the legendary investigative and civil rights reporter from Atlanta. He sported a loud sports jacket, flattop haircut, and sideburns that nearly came down to his chin. What I really noticed though, was the way he went after a story. It was "damn the torpedoes, full speed ahead."

As a fashion plate Jack evolved. But I was to learn that "full speed ahead" was about as close to idling as Jack ever got.

I think that juggernaut metabolism was the key to his success as a reporter. He went at sources so hard and he was so sure they would answer his questions that they often seemed too stunned *not* to talk. To an awed apprentice like me, it was almost hypnotic, watching the way he got people to talk.

In May 1970, he was dispatched from the Washington bureau to Kent State, whirling into town the morning after National Guardsmen had opened fire on antiwar protestors. I watched openmouthed as he balanced his Olivetti typewriter on a window ledge, cradled a telephone in his ear, and persuaded a campus police dispatcher to dictate the entire minute-by-minute radio log of the incident. It took quite a while to get it all down. I still wonder why the dispatcher didn't come to his senses and cut it off. He never did—he probably never thought he *could*.

Within hours, the FBI had sealed up the log and everything else. So as far as I know, the *Los Angeles Times* had the only official-source account of what the police and soldiers said and did before, during, and after the thirteen-second period in which almost seventy rounds were fired into the crowd, killing four students and wounding nine. It was a small moment in Jack's career, but it was not unique. As his deputy for twenty-one years after he became Washington bureau chief in 1975, I got to see his drive and his accomplishments up close. Both were large.

Jack Nelson would have been one of the most influential journalists of his era even if he had never come to Washington and become the *Los Angeles Times'* Washington bureau chief. As an investigative reporter for the *Atlanta Constitution* and then as the *Los Angeles Times'* correspondent for the Deep South, he had compiled an unparalleled record uncovering corruption in state and local government and documenting the violent repression of civil rights protests—exposés that positively affected many thousands of people.

As it happened, however, Jack's years in Washington continued his record of achievement, and he left enduring marks in several areas: his own work as a reporter, his success in expanding and strengthening the *L.A. Times* Washington bureau, and his untiring efforts to protect the rights of journalists. In all of these endeavors he was aided by becoming a nationally known figure in the Washington journalistic establishment.

His prominence grew in significant part because of the unique amplifying powers of television—powers he fully understood and exploited whenever possible in service of the paper he loved. His regular appearances on public television's *Washington Week in Review*, as well as on CNN, C-SPAN, and programs such as *Meet the Press*, made him a familiar figure to millions of people and won him legions of admiring fans. Thanks to his growing fame, Jack began to receive invitations to select briefings by senior government officials and to state dinners at the White House. A sociable man, he enjoyed these events. But the reporter in him saw them primarily as a means of expanding his contacts and boosting the bureau.

When Jack first assumed the position of bureau chief, the paper was still struggling for recognition in the capital. People on the East Coast almost never saw it, so it was easy to discount the stories we broke. But Jack's growing prominence rubbed off on the bureau. For us reporters, it meant our calls got calls returned faster. When we couldn't get someone on the phone—say a comment was needed from CIA Director William Webster without which the story couldn't run—Jack would pick up the phone. Magically, the reporter's next call would go right through.

During his tenure, our reporters scored exclusive interviews with Presidents Carter, Reagan, and Clinton and enjoyed greater access to small briefings, background sessions, seats on cabinet secretaries' planes, and other opportunities that they had sometimes struggled to obtain in the past. These opportunities depended almost entirely on the perceived importance of the news organization, not the individual reporter.

If anyone doubted that Jack had arrived, his invitation to serve on the presidential debate panel in 1976—the first televised debate since Kennedy squared off against Nixon in 1960—offered proof. A very big deal in the days before wall-to-wall debates, it was the kind of invitation reserved for those seen to be belonging to the first rank of national journalists. Jack's place in that elite group gave added validity to the *Los Angeles Times'* claim to have become a major national newspaper—in the eyes of official Washington as well as in the eyes of the paper's senior executives and members of the Chandler family, who owned it. That in turn increased Jack's leverage to grow the budget and expand the Washington bureau, elevate its status, and increase its impact. It also increased his ability to play an influential role outside the *L.A. Times*, in Harvard's prestigious Nieman Fellowship program, for example, and as cofounder of the Reporters Committee for Freedom of the Press.

Jack's fame, his entrée, naturally brought him a measure of personal satisfaction. He had come a long way from that cabin in the woods of Alabama, with its ditch and its pine root. It also enabled him to become one of the most energetic and successful promoters of other people's careers in Washington. I've hardly known anyone who did so much to give other people chances. Hundreds of times, Jack picked up the phone and "got right on it" and stayed "right on it" until he'd found a way to help.

As personally rewarding and professionally useful as his prominence became, it was Jack's own reporting of the national scene that may have had the most lasting impact.

The Reporter

Almost everyone has a favorite Jack Nelson story. Jack's longtime friend and colleague in the bureau, Ronald J. Ostrow, loves to tell one that goes back to the early 1970s, before Jack became bureau chief. At the time, the Washington bureau was located on the corner of 17th Street and Pennsylvania Avenue. That gave it a commanding view of the area in front of the White House and the Old Executive Office Building where many of the protests against the Vietnam War were staged.

One day, police instituted a heavy-handed crackdown on a large crowd of protesters, and the action was easily visible out of the bureau's floor-to-ceiling windows on the seventh floor. Jack, still a relatively new reporter in the bureau, grabbed a notebook and headed for the door.

"Why are you going down there? You can see everything from up here," a colleague shouted.

"No," Jack shouted back. "You can't get the badge numbers from up here."

Too impatient to wait for the elevator, he proceeded to plunge down seven flights of stairs and out into the action.

Just as he had in Georgia, Jack took the capital by storm. Often working in tandem with Ron, he turned out a stream of stories documenting the abuses of J. Edgar Hoover and his FBI—both reporters seemingly heedless of the personal and professional risks they ran. Watching Jack operate, I used to compare him to a guided missile. Once launched, he could not be deflected.

A man whose self-doubts—if he had any—were well concealed, Jack approached Washington in full confidence that he would succeed. He was aided in this by a relatively simple definition of his role, and the role of all journalists: people had a right to know what their government was doing; his job was to pry loose its secrets and publish them. As a guiding principle, that turned out to be as effective in Washington as it had been in confronting illegal gambling in Biloxi or the Ku Klux Klan in Alabama.

His brashness served him well. One of the near-sacred ground rules of the White House press corps, for instance, was that reporters not ask questions during "photo ops"—the brief moments when photographers were allowed in to an official meeting or event in order to take pictures. As Watergate heated up in 1972 and 1973, Jack crashed at least one Oval Office photo op and shouted pointed questions at President Nixon—an exercise he hoped would break down the aura of deference that had become one of the embattled president's best defenses. Unable to silence Jack, White House Press Secretary Ron Ziegler said disgustedly, "Don't worry, Mr. President. That's just Jack Nelson of the *Los Angeles Times*."

(Occasionally Jack went too far. Once he got so truculent with a secretary in the Reagan White House who he thought was blocking his access to her boss that he reduced her to tears. Afterwards, he felt so remorseful that he sent her a box of chocolates, prompting Jody Powell, who had been Jimmy Carter's press secretary, to crack that Jack was the only bureau chief in town with a line item in the budget for candy to mollify tearful secretaries.)

Jack also benefited from his reputation as someone who played straight with everyone. In 1977, shortly after President Carter returned from his historic Camp David summit with the leaders of Israel and Egypt, Jack was invited to a small private dinner at the White House for publishers, editors, and their wives. An ebullient Carter talked in great detail, clearly off the record, about what had occurred. Seated not far from the president, Jack would listen closely, occasionally darting into a nearby restroom to scribble notes, then returning to the table for more. Afterward, he asked Carter if he could write about what he had heard. Carter considered and then said, "Yes—just don't embarrass me." Jack did not embarrass Carter, but he did get an exclusive and revealing story about a president describing in his own words his reactions to a historic event—his frustrations with Menachem Begin, his growing closeness to Anwar Sadat.

In the fall of 1972, Jack broke what in terms of impact may have been the most important story he ever wrote. It involved Watergate, and it may have had a bearing on the course of history.

The previous summer, as George McGovern pursued his luckless quest against Richard Nixon, an alert security guard made a startling discovery in the Watergate apartment building: a small group of men was inside the headquarters of the Democratic National Committee with what appeared to be electronic listening devices. Most of the men were Cuban, but what they were doing and who they were doing it for was a mystery.

Republicans dismissed the episode as a low-level rogue operation and, since the facts were few and inconclusive, the episode might well have been forgotten except for a series of explosive stories by the *Washington Post*'s intrepid team of Bob Woodward and Carl Bernstein. Only the *Los Angeles Times* followed the *Post* into the fray during those first few months. Urged on by Edwin O. Guthman, the paper's national editor, the Washington bureau assigned Jack, Ron, and Robert L. Jackson to investigate full-time.

Still, the newspaper did not give their exclusives as much prominence as the *Post* gave its Watergate stories. As the weeks and months went by, the lack of aggressive coverage by most outlets, including the *New York Times*, the determined but restrained coverage by the *L.A. Times*, and the *Post*'s heavy reliance on anonymous sources combined to make it hard for citizens to understand what had actually happened and what the significance was. There was a very real possibility that the Watergate story might simply fade away.

That's when Jack shook things up.

Acting on a tip from Ron Ostrow, Jack discovered that there was an eyewitness to the break-in: an ex-FBI agent named Alfred Baldwin, whose job it was to monitor what was said inside the DNC and to deliver the recordings to the headquarters of the Nixon reelection campaign committee. The committee was presided over by no less a presidential insider than former Attorney General John Mitchell. Soon, other reporters had sniffed out Baldwin as well, some even offering to pay for an interview. But Jack—in what was clearly one of the most important selling jobs of his career—persuaded Baldwin and his lawyers that he should tell his story exclusively to the *Los Angeles Times*, for no money, in the form of a first-person, as-told-to-Jack-Nelson account.

The Baldwin account was printed on October 5, 1972. "It was powerful stuff . . . perhaps the most important Watergate story so far, because it was so tangible, it had an eyewitness, and it brought Watergate to the very door of the White House," David Halberstam wrote in his 1979 book *The Powers That Be*.

Now, it was no longer possible for Republicans to dismiss Watergate as an overblown figment of Democrats' partisan imaginations. Suddenly it was real. It was illegal. It had been directed from the top. And the details were supplied by a person who had been intimately involved in the operation, not some anonymous accuser whose knowledge and truthfulness could not be tested.

The scandal, of course, resulted in the first resignation of an American president, forced on Nixon by leaders of his own party, who knew that resigning was the only alternative to removal from office.

Watergate was such a colossal scandal, the misconduct by the president and his closest aides so blatant, that it might have been exposed and ended as it did even if Jack and his team at the *L.A. Times*, and Woodward and Bernstein at the *Post*, had not done what they did. It seems beyond dispute, however, that their reporting made that outcome inevitable. And the Baldwin story—coming so early, being so damning, and being so irrefutably sourced—was a foundation stone for what came after.

Jack would go on to produce dozens of other significant scoops during Watergate and hundreds of exclusives afterwards, but of all the stories he broke in Washington, the Baldwin piece undoubtedly had the widest impact.

The Bureau Chief

Jack never stopped reporting and writing, though he reluctantly gave up investigative reporting. It would have been too all-consuming, as he well knew. Instead, he changed his focus to political reporting, where, again, he worked his sources hard. His ties to Jimmy Carter and Bill Clinton and members of their senior staffs enabled him to break many exclusives. So did his long-standing relationships with political operatives and top figures in Ronald Reagan's administration. Jack also took the lead in covering such events as major presidential speeches, foreign summit meetings and such—a traditional role the *Times* expected its bureau chief to play.

Inevitably, though, once he became bureau chief, he devoted more of his time and energy to raising the bureau's profile, expanding its size and working to extend the impact of its reporting. That effort, which he pursued tirelessly, got results. One of Jack's devices for raising the bureau's profile was the bureau breakfast, where an array of Washington movers and shakers sat down with the *Times*' Washington reporters to answer questions for an hour or more. By dint of personal determination, Jack persuaded more and more prominent figures to attend these breakfasts. At receptions and other public events, he would corner cabinet secretaries, White House aides, presidential hopefuls and other movers, not letting them up for air until they had accepted the invitation. (We used to joke that the fifteen most dreaded words in Washington were "Senator, can I get you up to the bureau for a breakfast some time?")

Joking aside, over a period of more than a decade, the paper reaped a rich harvest of good stories, even breaking news that other news outlets would have to follow.

The breakfasts developed their own in-house legends, most notably an early visit by Senator Hubert H. Humphrey. At that time, the bureau served only an informal continental breakfast, little more than coffee, sweet rolls, and juice. Humphrey strode into the bureau early one morning, surveyed the modest fare, and with characteristic ebullience, declared: "Breakfast? Breakfast? You call this breakfast? Where are my bacon and eggs?"

One look from Jack and the bureau's office manager, the young but resourceful Mary Pat Kelly, darted away—returning miraculously with huge platters of scrambled eggs, bacon, and hash brown potatoes. Humphrey and his hosts tucked into the kind of breakfast he said his wife,

Muriel, served him every morning. And from then on, the *Times'* bureau breakfasts were meals to be reckoned with.

Before long, Jack saw another way to magnify the breakfasts' impact—by inviting in C-SPAN. At that time, cable news was still in its infancy, and C-SPAN's audience was miniscule. But C-SPAN's founder, Brian Lamb, was starved for fresh content. That created symbiotic possibilities for the network and the bureau, which Jack was quick to realize. In turn, the presence of the cameras helped attract increasingly top-drawer guests to the breakfasts. While there, they were able to look around and see what a powerhouse the bureau had become.

Jack simply never stopped flogging the paper or promoting its reporters, whatever the platform. When it came to the joint *Washington Post–Los Angeles Times* News Service, which distributed the work of both staffs to more than two hundred papers across the United States, he was constantly on the offensive. Since the *L.A. Times* was based on the West Coast and had a later deadline, the *Post* version of a story would likely reach the wire service editors first—which meant the *Post's* story was more likely to be sent out to subscribing papers. So Jack would continually urge his reporters to work faster and file sooner so that they would be the ones whose stories appeared in the "hometown" papers of elected officials in Washington.

The news service also enabled *Post* reporters and editors to see everything the *L.A. Times* bureau wrote before publication. (Remember, this was before the days of the Internet and newspaper websites.) That made it easy for *Post* editors and reporters to see a *Times* story and match it for the next morning's paper without necessarily giving the *Times* credit. Jack would become irate whenever that happened, and he had several impassioned conversations with Ben Bradlee, the *Post's* editor, protesting the "theft" of the bureau's work.

Given the diminished state of Washington newspaper bureaus in the present century, it's hard to conceive of the size and scale of operations of the major newspaper bureaus in the 1970s, 1980s, and the early 1990s—or of the exalted status of a Washington bureau chief. This was the heyday of newspapers, when print still set the national agenda, and bureau chiefs like Jack were the most influential journalists in town. His counterparts at the other major print outlets—giants like Hedrick Smith and Max Frankel of the *New York Times*, Al Hunt of the *Wall Street Journal*, Walter Mears of the Associated Press, Mel Elfin of *Newsweek*—likewise presided over the growth of large, powerful enterprises.

When Jack took over in the midseventies, the *L.A. Times* bureau had a total of seventeen reporters and editors, no photo staff, and only the most rudimentary library and other support facilities. At its peak, under his leadership, the bureau had a staff of fifty-seven, including two staff photographers, a full-scale photo lab, and three librarians. At one point, it even had a special computer installation and a staff that created its own federal campaign spending data bases. This unit produced reports that not even the Federal Election Commission could equal at the time.

The scale of the bureau's coverage in those days was even more mammoth by twenty-first-century standards. In Jack's day, we had three people assigned to the White House alone, and we routinely dispatched a dozen or more reporters to Moscow, Geneva, Paris, or Tokyo to cover summit meetings. Our team would blanket these events, filling as many as four or five full pages inside the paper, as well as a good chunk of page one. Such coverage regularly equaled or exceeded that of the *New York Times* and the handful of other papers still playing the journalistic equivalent of the Great Game.

Years afterward, Jack often referred to that period as a Golden Age. And he was the right person in the right place at the right time to reap its benefits. As Jack recounted in his memoir, Otis Chandler, the *Times* publisher and scion of the family that controlled the paper, was committed to building a world-class newspaper. So at the time when Jack came to Washington, the *Times* had both the will and the means to play for the gold ring.

The transformation of the Washington bureau had actually begun a few years earlier with the hiring of Robert J. Donovan as bureau chief. Donovan, who had headed the *New York Herald Tribune* bureau, was one of the most respected journalists in the capital. Thanks to his hires, the bureau was already producing some of the very best reporting in Washington before Jack became bureau chief. A main difference was that he made our coverage—and the paper—more widely recognized. The *L.A. Times* became a force that officials were more reluctant to ignore, and in the cold calculus of Washington, the bureau was treated accordingly, to the benefit of its reporting.

The First Amendment Champion

Jack was proud of his profession and always viewed journalism as a force for good. He believed, fervently, that an unfettered press was crucial to the well-being of the nation. As a result, he was dedicated heart and soul to the cause of protecting journalists' rights and privileges. But those rights and privileges came under assault by the Nixon administration, and prosecutors all over the country began issuing a barrage of subpoenas, demanding that reporters disclose their sources and turn over their notes.

An immediate cause for concern in 1970 was a *New York Times* reporter named Earl Caldwell, who had been covering the Black Panthers. The FBI not only wanted his notes; they also were demanding that he tell them anything and everything he could about possible illegal activity on the part of the Panthers.

Jack was among a group of thirty reporters who met to discuss the situation at the Georgetown Law Library. After the meeting, he, Fred Graham, and Tony Lukas, both with the *New York Times,* got together and came up with a name for their new organization: The Reporters Committee for Freedom of the Press. They put out a press release, and the Reporters Committee was born.

Over the years, it has provided legal assistance to thousands of reporters, free of charge, while pressing for passage of a strong shield law at the federal level that would recognize the right of reporters to protect their confidential sources. Jack had an active hand in guiding the committee for years, and even after he stepped down, he was always available to help. As Lucy Dalglish, who served as executive director for twelve years, said at Jack's memorial:

"While many journalists have helped to make us strong over the years, Jack stands alone.

"If we had a personnel problem, Jack took care of it.

"No money to pay the rent? Jack went to Charles Overby at the Freedom Forum and convinced him that there was nothing he'd like to do more than to pay our rent for ten years.

"Do you need testimony on the Hill or an affidavit for a court case? Jack was there."

In 1996, after more than two decades at the helm of the *Los Angeles Times* Washington bureau, Jack at last stepped down. His successor as bureau chief, Doyle McManus, would maintain and sometimes exceed the old standard, but what lay ahead was a war of attrition. Jack's timing, as always, was flawless.

Index